Steve

Merry ꓳ̶ tmas

with yours x.x

Defaced in order to be suitable for passing onto others who might enjoy it ! Instead of winging its way back to Amazon :) x.

Hee hee...

Airline Scams & Scandals

Airline Scams & Scandals

Edward Pinnegar

Sir Freddie Laker
may be at peace with his maker
but he is persona non grata
with IATA.

– HRH Prince Philip, Duke of Edinburgh

First published 2012

The History Press
The Mill, Brimscombe Port
Stroud, Gloucestershire, GL5 2QG
www.thehistorypress.co.uk

British Library Cataloguing in Publication Data.
A catalogue record for this book is available from the British Library.

ISBN 978 0 7524 6625 5

Typesetting and origination by The History Press
Printed in Great Britain

Contents

Mini-Scams

Main Stories

Introduction and Acknowledgements

Unfortunately for the aviation industry, it has, for some reason, had far in excess of its fair share of scams, scandals and incidences of general stupidity. Yet somehow nobody has properly documented these antics, which for the most part are rather amusing due to the silliness or naïveté of their protagonists; the people featured in this book thought that they could make a name for themselves in the aviation world – and most of them did, but for entirely the wrong reasons (that is, after all, why you are reading this now). In usually cringeworthy ways, they landed themselves in extremely awkward situations... sometimes quite literally!

Many of the stories within are, of course, quite controversial and every effort has been made to ensure their accuracy. Some of the stories are so truly absurd that they border on unbelievable – however, I assure you that they are all quite true. Although a concise bibliography has been included at the end of the book, the overall list of sources is too lengthy to include but can be provided following a request in writing to the publisher.

It would have been impossible to have put this book together without the help of others. Of course the subjects of the stories within the book require thanks for giving me something to write about – for both on occasions behaving utterly idiotically and for sometimes being too clever for their own good.

Many thanks must also go to my parents for their full support of the project (even after I explained the slightly more controversial side of the book), as well as all at Charterhouse: Hari Sood for typing a paragraph and putting up with my endless questions of 'does this sound right' and 'do you think I can get away with *that*?'; Seb Wadia for telling me about the dismal failure which was the Zambian attempt to get to Mars; Dan Federer and Chris McGleughlin for asking to be in the acknowledgements and SCA and SPMA for their support and for taking numerous bulky envelopes to the post office!

The following must also be thanked for their contribution in terms of photographs and illustrations: James Gordon, Richard Hunt, Leonid V. Kruzhkov, the *Northern Echo*, John Murphy, Peel Group, the Press Association and Zimin Vasily.

Without Pam Ann (aka Caroline Reid, comedienne) and her truly outrageous foreword, this book also wouldn't be what it is. Her PA, Emilio Barba, was equally generous – even after I told him in an email that my budget was nigh on non-existent, he and Pam Ann kindly went ahead with it anyway and the slightly mad foreword is the result.

Thanks are also due to the PPRuNe community for numerous suggestions as to what to include as well as what not to, and also to The History Press.

The stories in this book come from a variety of sources, websites and newspapers. The stories are all correct to the best of my knowledge; I sincerely hope I have not inadvertently offended anybody and would request that if you have any comments you contact me care of the publisher.

Foreword
by Pam Ann

Welcome aboard bitches!

My name is Pam Ann and I will be your head purser on this flight of scams and scandals. In the event of an emergency karaoke, microphones will fall from the unit above your head, pull down firmly, place over your nose and mouth and sing normally before attempting to help your children.

I am thrilled to be writing this foreword for Edward Pinnegar. He approached me after flying with me from New York JFK to London Heathrow – after all, I am an international air hostess to the stars and beyond (aka Australian comedienne Caroline Reid). I guide people through the conundrums of air travel, skewer the quirks of some of the biggest international airlines, mix up a stiff cocktail of camp, humour and glamour, and mine the dark side of fabulous in my live shows. Madonna, Elton and Cher have all flown with me – now Eddie (as I like to call him) joins my celebrity list of frequent flyers.

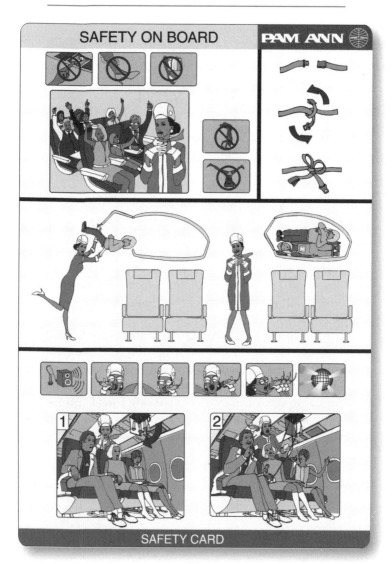

SAFETY ON BOARD

DIVERSITY MANAGEMENT - bill@diversitym.com.au

www.pamann.com

artwork: www.flindtdesign.dk

SAFETY CARD

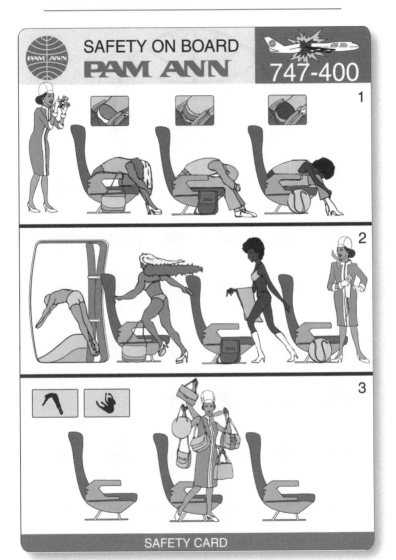

Eddie has been interested in airlines since he was flying high as a baby, screaming his way to the tiny island of Alderney in the Channel Isles, on a tiny Aurigny plane where the pilot turns around to give the safety briefing, and your dog can sit next to you for a child's fare. Now you won't get that on my airline; I charge economy passengers to breathe and nail their hands to the armrests.

Edward has flown with me since he was a baby and trust me, he never cried on my flights – I always put a little something in his milk. My tolerance with children is limited. Eddie loves and knows so much about the airline industry, I shouldn't take credit… but I will! I was the main inspiration for him penning this fabulous book on *Airline Scams and Scandals*; after all he has seen it all flying on Pam Ann Airlines. Gosh if my cabin walls could talk! If Ryanair's walls could talk they would scream 'HELP!' Eddie once asked me if I had heard about the Mile High Club. What he didn't realise was that I actually founded it in 1975 with Bob Marley, who then went on to pen a small song called

No Woman, No Cry. So, I've inspired many writers and artists in my years of flying.

He's quite a smarty-pants actually; he almost knows more than I do about flying. He tells many stories in this scandalous book, including everything from the Great Plane Robbery (which I hadn't heard of) to how Richard Branson joined the club which I founded.

I love a good read in between flights or on a back to back. I am always stuck for things to pass the time with and Eddie's books are so easy to read and not too long which I love as my attention span is limited. He is very funny too... I'd better be careful because there is always someone younger and hungrier coming down the spiral staircase (on a 747-8) behind you.

Buckle up and enjoy your flight.

Love Pam Ann
X

(www.pamann.com)

Mini-Scams

Easyjet's Idea of Kosher pork...

When Easyjet announced a new route from London Luton to Tel Aviv (capital city of Israel, a country where 76 per cent of the population are Jewish) in 2010, it also unveiled a special kosher menu designed by Hermolis of London, to be priced at the same rates as standard ranges on other flights.

However, in February 2011, many Jewish passengers were somewhat taken aback when the inflight offering included bacon baguettes and ham melts. The airline claimed that the wrong food canisters had been loaded at Luton. But when the same thing happened two weeks later, Easyjet was forced to offer an official apology as well as issue staff with reminders as to the requirements of many passengers travelling to and from the Holy Land.

Obviously shocked, David Abrahams of St John's Wood said, 'they shouldn't do this on a flight to Tel Aviv'.

British Bareways: trolley dollies take off... their clothes

You wouldn't usually associate the British flag carrier with saucy cabin crew – in fact it is quite excusable to assume precisely the opposite (in September 2011, a drunk BA passenger on a flight from Phoenix was jailed for three months for calling one of the cabin crew 'sexy' – he later admitted to being 'ashamed' of his behaviour). However, when a set of naughty snaps appeared online in 2010, they spread around the internet like wildfire... latterly ending up on a porn website.

The photos included stewardesses lifting their skirts and lying in overhead lockers in suggestive poses. A source at

BA said: 'They were never intended to get out and it would never have occurred to the girls they would end up on a porn site.'

However, British Bareways has remained cagey about the incident and insists that there is no evidence that the subjects of the shots actually worked for the airline – they may just be wearing BA uniforms (complete with cravats) and identification cards whilst posing in surprisingly similar aircraft as an impersonation... really?

Stuff the UN: sanctions weren't going to stop Air Rhodesia!

When Rhodesia declared unilateral independence from Great Britain in November 1965, it did not necessarily appreciate what would ensue. By December 1966, the United Nations had taken an historic step in its twenty-one-year history and resorted to mandatory economic sanctions in an attempt to bring down Ian Smith's white minority government. The sanctions declared an international embargo on 90 per cent of Rhodesia's exports whilst prohibiting the 122 member states from selling oil, arms, cars or aircraft to the country or to provide it with any form of 'financial or other economic aid'.

A year before Smith signed the UDI, the national flag carrier had just been formed. Air Rhodesia was a subsidiary of Central African Airways and by 1964 had several Vickers Viscounts (a medium-sized British turboprop aircraft) as well as a couple of Douglas Dakotas. Two BAC One-Elevens (passenger jets, again British) were due but after the declaration of independence these went to Zambian Airways instead.

By 1973, the airline was looking to expand and it had its eye on three ex-Calair Boeing 720s which were sitting idle with a European dealer at Basle Airport in Switzerland. However, due to the sanctions any such sale would have been prohibited. So, a front organisation was formed in Paraguay which went through with the sale and paid the dealer in US dollars.

Boeing-qualified freelance crews arrived shortly afterwards, and flew them together to Las Palmas (Canary Islands) where they made a refuelling stop, paid for the fuel in cash, and filed flight plans for the three aircraft across the South Atlantic to Paraguay, departing in the evening. Fictitious position reports were sent by HF radio as if the aircraft were flying south and, needless to say, the 720s did not arrive in Paraguay but instead at Salisbury (now Harare) later the next morning. The aircraft subsequently formed the jet fleet of Air Rhodesia for the remaining years of UDI, and again for several years as Air Zimbabwe.

African 747: when the crew did a runner...

Sometime in the 1990s, a Nigerian 747 operator sent an aircraft to Europe for heavy maintenance. It was to be flown by an Asian crew, who were given a briefcase with cash to pay the maintenance operator as the airline had something of a dubious reputation.

The aircraft was delivered to the overhaul facility as promised, but crew, briefcase and several thousand US dollars disappeared, never to be seen again – firmly bucking the national stereotype; a Nigerian airline got scammed!

When the airline didn't pay, Guernsey Police arrested (not impounded) one of its aircraft. (Richard Hunt)

Arrest the Plane the innovative way of making a Guernsey airline pay up

When Guernsey-based operator Air Sarnia applied to take on the long-standing Aurigny Air Services on several routes in and around the Channel Islands during 1989, it did not appreciate what it was letting itself in for – a war of attrition. Both airlines sustained heavy losses, and Air Sarnia could only keep flying by not paying all its fees.

By May 1990, the airline owed Alderney and Guernsey airports more than £8,800 in landing and parking fees. The States of Guernsey (the government) decided to take action, and on the 11th of that month Guernsey police 'arrested' an Air Sarnia aircraft: they chose to arrest – not impound – the aircraft, rather than its pilot, occupants or anyone associated with the airline. Jersey authorities were having similar problems but decided to be slightly more sensible about the matter...

Rerouting Accidently on Purpose the longer way from Malta to Vienna

Air traffic management delays sometimes need novel solutions. Some thirty years ago, Austrian Airlines came up with a very effective one. Usually, the Malta–Vienna flight would have to go through Italian airspace – an absolute black hole for delays. On one notable occasion, things got so bad that the flight had to file for Amsterdam, setting off southwards to Tunisia and then through Algeria and Morocco, then north up through Spain and France and when overhead Paris, refiling for Vienna. This would cost thousands of schillings more but the flight got there in the end!

Avoiding the Queue innovative ways of getting round work-to-rule delays

In the early 1970s when Frankfurt air traffic control decided to stage industrial action (in the form of work to rule), this caused horrific delays and most aircraft were held up for at least an hour... a sticky situation which called for an innovative solution.

Because the parking was out of view of the ground controller, as soon as the aircraft was on the ground certain pilots called for start clearance knowing it would not be given for a good 45 minutes. It wasn't long before air traffic control cottoned on and refused to put an aircraft in the queue until it was confirmed that the doors were closed. They thought they had put an end to these antics. They were wrong.

Some BEA pilots decided they could outwit the Frankfurters and devised a new ploy – when asked if their doors were closed, an absolutely hand-on-heart confirmation could be given... they hadn't landed yet! So when the reply came back (for example) 'Bealine 123, roger that, you are number seventy-two in the start sequence' (i.e. there are seventy-one aircraft in the queue before you), the pilot would be perfectly happy as the aircraft would arrive at its parking slot, offload passengers, refuel and take on the next load of passengers, by which time their turn had come and off they went. When air traffic control discovered this latest tactic, they were distinctly unamused – as you would probably expect a Frankfurter to be when he discovers some crafty Brits have been mucking him around.

Fake Crash: how to boost TV viewing numbers

If you were walking down Avenue Atwater in Montreal, Canada, on the morning of 25 March 2010, a truly horrific sight would have greeted you. In a parking area just opposite the Bell Centre, a bright yellow light aircraft sat nose down on a crumpled 4x4; the wreckage smouldering.

There was, however, a very good reason for this. It was all a publicity stunt, dreamt up by French language cable channel Canal D to promote its new television series on life-threatening close calls. 'It was not our intention to put people in danger,' explained Élise Beauchemin, director of communications. 'For us, it was just to create curiosity and suspense… we wanted to make it look very real.' They successfully achieved the latter aim – to the point where members of the public were flooding the emergency services with calls to report a plane crash.

Production crews had been up at 4a.m. that morning positioning the 'advertising sculpture', and spent the whole day pumping artificial smoke into the car (which then seeped out into the street) and explaining to the public about the new show. However, the stunt was somewhat counterproductive in the amount of criticism it received – a CBC poll revealed the extent to which the public were against the stunt, and many said that the television channel should be forced to pay for any money which it cost the emergency services through increased call numbers.

However, given that the police had been informed of the stunt, no action was taken. Viewing numbers certainly weren't bad, although it does seem a slightly odd way to promote a television show.

Loanshark: the £1 million flat which the head of Flybe put 'on the house'

When UK airline Flybe was floated on the London Stock Exchange in late 2010, a great deal of glossy bumf was produced for prospective investors. It went through the ins and outs of the airline in great detail – to extents which perhaps CEO Jim French might not necessarily have intended in some cases.

Page 228 of the 274-page prospectus made interesting reading – readers were told that in 2005, French was given an interest free, unsecured loan of £1 million from the main shareholder Rosedale Aviation Holdings in order to buy a property in London, where he reportedly spends much time on business. The flat in question is believed to be in Belgravia and the loan is repayable when he sells his shares in the company.

The prospectus also revealed that French walked away with a £715,000 pay package for the 2009/2010 financial year, which incidentally was £36,000 more than that of Willie Walsh, the CEO of British Airways at the time. The float also made Jim French's shares in Flybe worth something near £14 million... all evidence considered, you'd therefore certainly be excused for thinking that being the Flybe boss isn't such a bad job.

Waving Goodbye: stealing a plane in front of the police

Sheffield City Airport had a chequered history (see page 88) – having opened in 1997, it suffered major setbacks following the 9/11 atrocities and their subsequent repercussions. By 2005, its future was in doubt as the airlines serving it (BA, KLM, Aer Arann, Sabena and Albion Air) had all pulled out for various reasons.

This left only a couple of pilot training companies and some private aircraft owners. One such training company claimed to offer cut-price tuition and ground schooling for airline pilot students. However, by 2008 it too had run into financial difficulties, and was served various notices regarding unpaid bills. Eventually, it got to the point where bailiffs were attempting to remove propellers from aircraft.

Reportedly, the company boss decided he would take them head on – so on 21 May 2008 he rocked up at Sheffield City Airport (which had officially closed for the last time on 30 April – and had already reopened officially as a business park) and managed to fly out an impounded Piper Cherokee whilst being chased down the runway by several cops. After he had taken off, he even gave the South Yorkshire Police a goodbye wing-waggle, although it is unlikely that they saw it because they were on the phone to Doncaster Radar asking them to track his movements.

Conflicting reports said that he had flown to Sturgate Airfield in Lincolnshire where the training company owed a maintenance company money, and also that the aircraft was later sighted together with some others the training company also owned at Bagby Airfield in North Yorkshire.

Either way, it was eventually discovered (and stripped of radios and anything else of value), the company soon folded and the boss was banned from taking part in any company management for seven years. He is allegedly currently trying to set up a new flight training school with ambitions to train 600 pilots each year – far more than the largest academies in the UK at present. The project has yet to come to fruition.

Cattle Class: some of the odder items brought to check-in

What do dead cows, tarantulas and wheels of cheese all have in common? You might answer that they could all feature in slightly warped (perhaps substance-induced) nightmares. In fact, they are all things which Virgin Atlantic staff have been presented with at the check-in desk. One lady even turned up at New York's JFK Airport with family members carrying her bath, which they hadn't even bothered to package or wrap.

A couple who fell in love on the island of Grenada in the Caribbean decided they needed a memento... so appeared at check-in with a bag of seawater and Grenadian sand. Another person turned up expecting to be allowed to board with a car engine in its entirety...

So next time you consider what a boring job it must be to work on the check-in desks, think again!

Blind Ignorance how S7 discriminates against disabled passengers

If you are visually impaired and want to fly with S7 Airlines in Russia, you may encounter some difficulties. Pavel Obiukh was due to fly from Kazan on a business trip in February 2009 (ironically as a member of the regional non-governmental organisation of people with disabilities, Perspektiva), but was not allowed to board because he was visually impaired – even though he had informed the airline about his disability previously.

Pavel stresses that when his company booked the ticket, he also asked his colleagues to tell the air carrier about his disability in advance. They did, but apparently to no avail – when he turned up at the airport a member of staff claimed he would not be allowed to board.

But Pavel's case is no exception. Summer 2008 saw another member of Perspektiva, Natalia Prisetskaya, who uses a wheelchair, wanting to fly to Vladikavkaz in Russia's Caucasus. She was also denied access unless she was with an accompanying person. On that occasion, S7 was punished. The court ordered the airline to pay 50,000 roubles in compensation, as well as fining the company a further 25,000 roubles, with half of that to be paid to the Consumers' Confederation. But S7 clearly weren't going to be told.

Main Stories

The Ultimate Skywayman: flying 1 million miles without tickets

No book on airline scams and scandals would be anywhere near complete without at least a mention of Frank Abagnale.

As the subject of the 2002 film *Catch Me if You Can*, Abagnale was portrayed by Leonardo DiCaprio and it is probably fair to say that he owes much of his fame to this. Having started forging cheques aged sixteen, he continued to do so for the next five years in no fewer than twenty-six different countries – a scam worth $2.5 million on its own. But added to his other scams, the cheque forgeries almost fade into insignificance.

Abagnale was one of four children, and up to his mid-teens the family lived in Bronxville in New York. However, when aged sixteen his world was turned upside down – his French mother (Paulette) divorced his father; later, he would be the only child of whom his father would gain custody. In his autobiography, Abagnale claimed that his father was a major role model for him, but he felt that his

Frank Abagnale had fraud down to a fine art. (Marcus JB)

father did not necessarily want him, and attempts to reunite the family until his father's death in 1974 were unsuccessful.

And it was his father who was his first con victim: having given his son a petrol station credit card so he could commute to his part-time job, he found a rather nasty bill. His son was turning into a popular young man, and had to finance his dates somehow, so he made a deal with petrol station attendants that he would 'buy' various car-related items like tyres and batteries, but they would then give him cash and keep the items. Ultimately, this meant that he was getting cash off a petrol station credit card whilst the bills were still relating to what the card was given to him for. Several thousand dollars later, his father called a halt to the scheme.

He then moved onto writing cheques on overdrawn accounts – however, this too could only work for a limited time because the bank eventually requested payment. So he assumed multiple identities and opened different accounts at different banks. Another method he experimented with was printing his account number on blank deposit slips, and then adding them to the stack of real blank slips on the counter in the bank – this meant that the deposits written on the slips by customers ended up going into his account rather than that of the legitimate recipients.

Smaller and more opportunistic tricks were also employed. For example, on one occasion Abagnale noticed where airlines would drop off their daily collections of cash. Contained in zip-up bags, these would be deposited in a drop box at the airport. Abagnale thus bought a security guard's uniform at a local costume shop and put up a sign on the drop box saying something along the lines of 'out of service, place all deposits with security guard on duty'. This way, he was able to impersonate the security guard and collect the money. At lectures since, he has expressed incredulity that anyone could believe that a drop box was 'out of order'.

Soon, he got into airlines. Between the ages of sixteen and eighteen, he pretended to be a Pan Am pilot and flew more than 1 million miles on 250 flights to twenty-six different countries by deadheading; a process by which airline staff can fly for free to reach another location where they are required by the carrier. The added bonus to this was that he was able to stay for free in very good hotels, and food and drinks were billed to the airline. However, there was a problem. As a deadheading pilot sitting in the jump seat, he was often invited by real pilots to take the controls. Generally, he got around this by using the 'bottle-to-throttle' rule and saying that he had drunk too recently. However, on one occasion it would have been rude to turn the offer down so he sat down and engaged the autopilot; Abagnale recalled trying to not let his nerves show when he had 140 lives in his hands and yet he 'couldn't fly a kite'. At one point, he also took to forging Pan Am pay cheques so he was having his wages paid for doing nothing except for sleeping with air hostesses in upmarket hotels.

But airlines certainly weren't his only field of conning. Whilst still posing as a Pan Am pilot, he managed to get away with forging a Columbia University degree, and used it to teach sociology under a pseudonym at Brigham Young University for one term, working as a teaching assistant. He also managed to impersonate a chief paediatrician in a Georgia hospital (under yet another identity). However, becoming a doctor happened more by chance: after nearly being arrested disembarking a flight in New Orleans and afraid of possible capture, he moved temporarily to Georgia. When filling out an application for accommodation he impulsively listed his occupation as 'doctor', fearing that the owner might check with Pan Am if he wrote 'pilot'.

By coincidence, a real doctor who lived in another apartment told him that more supervisors were needed, and he could be one until better qualified individuals could be recruited. This was not difficult as supervisors did little real medical work – when this was required, he was able to fake his way through most of it by letting interns handle cases coming in during the night shifts, so he didn't have to involve himself with setting broken bones. After nearly a year, the hospital found a replacement and Abagnale moved on as soon as possible – principally because he nearly allowed a baby to die from oxygen deprivation. Realising that he could put lives at risk, he returned to Pan Am.

But 'working' at the airline still wasn't enough for him. Whilst posing as First Officer Robert Black, he forged a Harvard University law transcript, and on his third attempt passed the bar exam of Louisiana. This got him a job at the Louisiana Attorney General's office – at the age of just nineteen. All this was a stroke of luck, as a Pan Am stewardess who he was dating at the time (there were many) told Abagnale that a friend of hers said the bar needed more lawyers. After producing a fake transcript from Harvard, he did his best to prepare himself for the compulsory entrance exam. On his third attempt, he passed the bar exam legitimately after eight weeks of hard grind over the law books; thankfully, he was allowed as many tries as he needed so he eventually succeeded through a process of elimination.

Fortunately, all his job generally entailed was fetching coffee and books for his boss. Unfortunately, there was a real Harvard graduate who also worked there and Abagnale found himself constantly bombarded with questions about his time at Harvard. Because he could not answer any of them, he resigned after eight months to protect himself; the suspicious graduate had been making inquiries into his background.

But Abagnale's luck wouldn't last forever. In 1969, aged twenty-one, an Air France air stewardess who he had dated recognised him and tipped off the police. He was arrested, and twelve different countries sought his extradition. After a two-day trial in France, he served six months in Perpignan where he was held nude in a tiny, filthy, lightless cell that he was never allowed to leave. It lacked any kind of toilet facilities, a mattress (or even a blanket), and access to food and water was severely restricted.

He was then deported to Sweden, where he served six months in a rather better prison in Malmö. Meanwhile, a Swedish judge had persuaded the US State Department to revoke his passport – and without this, Swedish authorities were legally compelled to deport him to the USA. Here, he was sentenced to a further twelve years in a federal prison for multiple counts of forgery. But his extradition to that country had not gone entirely to plan: after landing at New York in a BOAC Vickers VC10, he managed to escape onto a taxiway and over a fence. He caught a taxi to the Bronx where he changed clothes and picked up the keys to a safe in Montreal which contained $20,000.

With the intention of flying from Montreal to São Paulo, Brazil (a country with which the USA had no extradition treaty at the time) having collected the money, he set off to Canada by train. However, on arrival there, whilst standing in a ticket queue he was spotted by a Canadian police constable and was handed over to the US Border Patrol. He then began his twelve-year jail sentence, but managed to obtain huge privileges in the prison by assuming the identity of an undercover prison inspector. The part of Abagnale's (ghost-written) autobiography regarding his time in prison makes an interesting read, and includes two successful escapes; given that it is not strictly relevant to airline scams or scandals, it shouldn't be spoilt here.

After serving less than five years, he was released on condition that he would help federal authorities (without remuneration) with crimes committed by frauds and scammers. Because his family was now all but broken, he did not wish to return to New York and was paroled in Texas instead. Because he was not paid in this capacity, he tried several jobs including being a cook, a grocer, and latterly a film projectionist. However, he was fired from each of these for failing to tell his employers about his previous convictions. Finding these jobs both unfulfilling and frustrating, he approached a bank and offered to speak to their staff about fraud techniques. If they did not find it helpful then they would pay him nothing, but if they did then he would earn $500 and have his name recommended to other banks. This was hugely successful, and he later founded Abagnale & Associates. As a consultancy firm, it specialises in advising businesses on fraud and scams and so far more than 14,000 companies and businesses have implemented his fraud prevention program.

Today, Abagnale continues to work with the FBI and is one of their longest-serving consultants after working with them for nearly forty years. He teaches at the FBI Academy and lectures throughout America on the subject of fraud within business. And, it seems, he is one of the only people in this book to have been caught up in enough scams and scandals to serve time for them – but then to come out of the experience all the better.

The Zambian Space Programme taking Christianity to Mars in a 44-gallon oil drum

It is unlikely that you have ever heard of the Zambian attempt to enter the space race – and for good reason: it never got off the ground (quite literally).

If you visited a 'secret location' around 7 miles from Lusaka in early 1964, you would have seen a man rolling some cats and a few people down a hill in an oil drum. You probably would have thought him mad. And you most likely wouldn't have been far from the truth. This secret location was the headquarters of Zambia's own (although it should be said that the project wasn't backed by the government) Academy of Sciences and Space Technology – in fact, it was apparently little more than an abandoned farmhouse.

The man who led this extraordinary 'organisation'? Edward Makuka Nkoloso was an independence activist and candidate for mayor of Lusaka who had great visions for his country. He envisaged that, 'if I had been elected, the capital city of Zambia would quickly have been another Paris, if not another New York... never mind, we will have our Paris yet.' He complained vociferously in a magazine article which he authored about the Independence Celebrations Committee suggesting that his idea to have Zambia 'burn with the blast of the academy's rocket being launched into space' would 'terrify the guests and possibly the whole population'... however, he did mention: 'I think they were worried about the dust and noise' which was 'a great pity'.

What made it worse was that he was all ready to go. He had several trainees including a missionary (who was specially instructed not to force Christianity on the primitive Martian natives) as well as a teenage would-be spacegirl called Martha Mwambwa (who had to be withdrawn from the programme because she became pregnant part-way through) who, dressed in British Army helmets and overalls, would be rolled down a hill in a 44-gallon oil drum to train them to become acclimatised to weightlessness. This oil drum would also be spun round a tree to show the prospective astronauts what space flight was like and they were also trained to walk on their hands, 'the only way humans can walk on the moon'.

These loyal people would, under plans set out by Nkoloso's academy (he was self-appointed director), launch off to Mars on Independence Day 1964 from the Independence Stadium in Lusaka, together with several cats (also specially trained) in a number of small rockets which at first sight apparently appeared similar to aluminium dustbins – although about 3m in length. Even the usually neutral news agency Reuters had doubts: one reporter declared after meeting Nkoloso that, 'To most Zambians, these people are just a bunch of crackpots. And from what I have seen today I'm inclined to agree.'

The only problems Nkoloso faced were 'a few difficulties with my own firing system, derived from the catapult' and also some trouble he was having with his space-men and space-women. 'They won't concentrate on space-flight; there's too much love-making when they should be studying the Moon' (this was early in the programme – he later focussed his ambitions on Mars).

Nkoloso also had some other pressing concerns, believing that both Russian and American spies were operating in Zambia. 'They are all trying to capture Martha and my cats. They want our space secrets.' He honestly thought he was six or seven years ahead of his competitors in terms of research... but except for those minor niggles there wasn't much holding the programme back. Oh, except two other things – a £7 million grant from UNESCO, and supplies of liquid oxygen and hydrogen from the US government. As neither of these requests were fulfilled, the project never got off the ground – rather lucky for these would-be astronauts: one worries about their safety at the mercy of Nkoloso, who had apparently taught science at primary school level previously. This experience had obviously helped: Zambia's population numbered just 3.6 million at the time, and with barely 1,500 African-born high school graduates and fewer than 100 college graduates, it would have been a struggle without it!

So that's why you've never heard of the Zambian space programme; it really was condemned to failure from the start.

Concordeeeeee: how naming the aircraft became a supersonic kerfuffle

Disappointingly for more romantic readers, Concorde's name came not from the lips of a gifted poet but from a quick browse of Roget's Thesaurus following an informal chat between a British Aircraft Corporation employee and his family. The first reaction: '... with the 'e', of course?' The answer was a hesitant 'Yes.' However, this question wasn't just going to make the family of this employee think. It would be a matter of contention between Britain and France for years to come – somewhat ironic considering it was meant to be symbolic of harmony, agreement and unity between the two nations.

The issue had arisen in part from a spat between Harold Macmillan and Charles de Gaulle, when the latter had offended the British PM by telling him on one visit that he had a cold and therefore couldn't see him. In response to this snub, Macmillan went and knocked off the 'e'. Touchy, one might think – but all went quiet for a while until, when he visited Toulouse in December 1967 for the rollout of the aircraft, Tony Benn (then Minister of Technology) announced that he was putting back the 'e' to undo an insult to the French which he didn't support anyway. He said, somewhat mischievously, in an article in *The Guardian* in October 2003: 'I didn't tell anybody I was planning to do it... once I had announced it in Toulouse, they couldn't do anything about it.'

This provoked a nationalist uproar which, luckily, subsided when he announced in a short speech that 'E stands for excellence, for England, for Europe and for the Entente Cordiale.' Because of this declaration, an irate nationalist Scotsman wrote in to a saying that 'You talk about 'e' for England, but part of it is made in Scotland.' He was right – Scotland had contributed nosecones for the aircraft, so Benn replied that it was 'e' for Écosse (the French name for Scotland) as well.

This fuss was unprecedented over something apparently so small – but it represented the staunch nationalist movement that still exists in the United Kingdom to this day. The 'e' in Concorde had caused an uproar – in his memoirs, Benn noted that it could for been 'e for extravagance and e for escalation [of costs] as well!'

In the end, that came to seven good reasons for an 'e' on the end – a most appropriate (but controversial) one, therefore.

Cessna in Red Square tricking Soviet nuclear defences in a light aircraft

The airspace surrounding Moscow during the Cold War was generally regarded as almost impregnable – it was one of the most tightly controlled areas in the world, to protect it against any potential Western aggression. Other than an

Mathias Rust defied the odds to land a Cessna 172 in Moscow's city centre. (Luca Diffuse)

incident regarding an American U2 reconnaissance aircraft in 1960 and the issue of a South Korean jumbo jet being shot down in 1983 for failing to respond whilst flying over restricted airspace in the east of the country, it took a lot of skill to get over unnoticed.

All that changed on 28 May 1987, when a West German teenager with just fifty hours of flying time under his belt decided to take an unauthorised flight under the radar from Helsinki to Moscow. On 13 May, Mathias Rust had set out on a small tour of northern Europe, flying a 1980 Cessna 172 (four-seater prop) which he had hired from his flying club for three weeks – no questions asked. He started out from Uetersen (near Hamburg) on a long flight to the Faroe Islands (via the Shetlands), followed by a week-long visit to

Iceland (where he visited Höfði House in Reykjavík, the site of the unsuccessful Reagan/Gorbachev summit in October 1986) followed by a stop in Bergen on his way back to Helsinki, where he arrived on the morning of 28 May.

Here, he filed a flight plan to Stockholm but after take-off he turned the 172 to the east and switched off all communications equipment. Air traffic control continued to attempt contact as he weaved around the airways, but he disappeared off Finnish screens near Sipoo.

A rescue effort was organised including a Finnish Border Guard patrol boat and an underwater search near an oil patch where the plane had supposedly gone down. Rust was later fined $100,000 for this rather expensive exercise. In the meantime, he had crossed the Baltic coastline and was headed for Moscow. At 2.30p.m., he appeared on military radar and three surface-to-air missiles tracked him for some time, but were not given permission to launch – partially because Soviet authorities thought that he was perhaps a lost student pilot.

However, air defences were readied and two fighter jets were sent to investigate. At 2.50p.m., flying near the town of Gdov, he was falsely identified as a Yakolev Yak-12 aircraft, which looks fairly similar to a 172 at a distance. However, because of icing and clouds he descended – and disappeared off the radar screens once again. Once the clouds had disappeared, Rust climbed back up to 2,500ft, and appeared on a radar screen in a new sector. Two more interceptors were sent to investigate.

Now nearly two hours into his flight, Rust said that the sun was shining when he saw 'a black shadow shooting in the sky and then disappear'. A few moments later, from out of a layer of clouds in front of him, an aircraft appeared. 'It was coming at me very fast, and dead-on,' Rust recalled. 'And it went whoosh! – right over me.' The aircraft in question was no less than a MiG-23 fighter jet, designed to fly at more than twice the speed of sound. Rust said afterwards that this was the moment when he started to ask himself: 'Is this when they shoot you down?' However, he wasn't aware that the MiG was having its own problems. Because it was meant to fly at such great speed and he was cruising along at just 130mph, it was having trouble not

Mathias Rust's aircraft now hangs from the roof of the German Museum of Technology in Berlin. (Andrey Belenko)

falling out of the sky. The nose was high and it had both flaps and landing gear extended... almost on the edge of a stall. The pilot gave no signals to Rust and it was only later that he was informed that the MiG pilot had been trying to contact him over the radio – on high-frequency military channels. In any case, the Cessna's radio was switched off.

After failing to contact him, the fighter pilot eyed him for a minute then retracted the wheels and flaps and accelerated off into two long arcs around Rust at about half a mile, before flying off into the distance. At 3p.m., Rust flew into a Soviet military training zone where between seven and twelve aircraft with similar characteristics to his own were involved in fairly basic training exercises including touch-and-go landings and straight and level flight.

He continued past Lake Seliger, now just 230 miles from Moscow – but appeared on yet another set of radar screens. Once again, two fighters were sent to intercept. However, given the low cloud base they considered it too risky to draw up alongside and visual contact was therefore never made. Later, whilst 40 miles west of Torzhok, another radar controller picked up Rust's aircraft but due to a search and rescue operation being performed by two helicopters at the time, he assumed that Rust's aircraft was one of them due to its similar radar signature.

So once again, Rust had managed to get away with it. He flew on, out of the Leningrad military zone and into that of Moscow. The handoff report from the Leningrad commander to Moscow officials said only that controllers had tracked a Soviet aircraft flying without its transponder (a kind of tracking device) turned on. Nothing more than that – no mention of the Gulf of Finland, no mention of a

West German registration, no mention of several fighter jets intercepting what was in fact a Cessna 172 heading straight for Moscow. Meanwhile, Rust was flying through the outer part of what was known as the 'Ring of Steel' – a set of defences to protect Moscow from any potential attack from even the most high-tech of aircraft.

Just after 6p.m., Rust reached Moscow. However, because at that time the city had very few tall buildings which a pilot could use to navigate, he found it fairly difficult to find the city centre. 'As I manoeuvred around, I sort of narrowed in on the core of the city,' he said. But then it came into view – the turreted walls of the Kremlin were distinctive enough for Rust to be able to immediately orientate himself. Turning towards it, he scanned the ground for a place to land.

He briefly considered landing inside the Kremlin wall, but discounted that plan as, although there was plenty of space, he was wary of what the KGB might do with him. 'If I landed inside the wall, only a few people would see me, and they could just take me away and deny the whole thing. But if I landed in the square, plenty of people would see me, and the KGB couldn't just arrest me and lie about it. So it was for my own security that I dropped that idea.'

So he circled and reconsidered. Between the Kremlin wall and the Hotel Russia, a six-lane-wide bridge with light traffic on it crossed the Moscow River and ran into the Red Square. Inspecting the bridge, Rust observed three sets of wires. He would have to drop under the first set and level out under the middle set, engine idling with full flap, before setting down on the bridge. It later turned out that there were usually many sets of wires but they had been removed that morning for maintenance – interrogators later told Rust how lucky he was; it was also Border Guards' Day so the border was likely to be less defended. He wasn't to know, but a set of extraordinary coincidences helped him on his way significantly.

Getting under the wires was not going to be the only challenge. He put down on the bridge, but then looked ahead only to realise that there was an old man in a probably equally ancient Volga car. Luckily, there was just enough space on the left to pass him. However, with such a small amount of space Rust was worried that when the driver noticed that he was being overtaken not by a car but by a light aircraft, he might swerve and crash into it. Luckily, the only reaction from the driver was a look of incredulity and disbelief.

He taxied through Red Square and pulled up outside St Basil's Cathedral, shut down the engine and heaved a sigh of relief. Then, expecting to be mobbed by KGB agents, he opened the door and stepped out of the aircraft. He leaned against the aircraft and waited. No, it wasn't Gorbachev's private aircraft. No, it wasn't a film set. It was a very idealistic West German teenager trying to prove his point. And that he had done, embarrassing a lot of people in the process.

After standing trial, Rust was locked up for breaching aviation rules and, bizarrely, for 'hooliganism'. He was released shortly afterwards as a goodwill gesture towards the West, as part of Mikhail Gorbachev's attempts to sweeten relations with Reagan and Thatcher. However, Gorbachev used Rust to his advantage in another way too. The signature policies of his government were *glasnost* (openness and transparency) and *perestroika* (restructuring); sweeping reforms. However, many of the 'old guard' in the Soviet military were firmly against them and Gorbachev was having an increasingly hard time with them. So Rust presented him with the opportunity to sack the people he disliked (on account of such an embarrassing mistake) and also push through reforms. This he did – Rust therefore helped Gorbachev to reform the country and, indirectly, ease relations with the West. Farfetched as the idea of landing a plane in Red Square to ease relations was, it therefore ended up doing just that.

The Great Plane Robbery: the only unsolved US airline hijacking in history

There was drizzle in the breezy air on that November afternoon forty years ago, when a man who identified himself as Dan Cooper turned up at the airport desk in a suit with a black briefcase and bought a one-way ticket on the thirty-minute flight from Portland, Oregon, to Seattle, Washington.

It would have been a normal flight for the other thirty-seven passengers and five crew on that Boeing 727 had he not passed a note to Flo Schaffner, the flight attendant seated nearest to him on a jumpseat. Assuming it to be the phone number of yet another lonely businessman, she put it unopened into her pocket. However, the next time she passed him he said, 'You'd better read that. I have a bomb,' looking at the briefcase on his lap.

The aircraft chosen by Dan Cooper for what has become one of the most infamous hijackings in US history. (John F. Ciesla)

Schaffner went to the galley and read the note, then showed it to fellow flight attendant Tina Mucklow. They hurried to the cockpit, where Captain Scott was informed. The pilot immediately radioed Seattle air traffic control, who alerted Seattle police, who in turn alerted the FBI. They then put through an urgent call to Northwest's president, Donald Nyrop, who ordered full compliance with Cooper's demands – no doubt he hoped to avoid the negative publicity that a disaster aboard a Northwest flight would bring.

The note asked for $200,000 in cash and two sets of parachutes (two backpacks and two chestpacks, which would serve as emergency backups). Cooper ordered the items to be delivered to the jet when it landed at Seattle, and he said he would blow up the plane if the airline failed to pay up and comply with his requests. Schaffner and others who read the note later agreed that it included the phrase 'no funny business' – Cooper had asked for it back because it was potential evidence.

The captain dispatched Schaffner back to Cooper, who had moved to the window seat. She sat in the aisle seat and he opened the briefcase just wide enough to reveal some wires and two red sticks which could have been dynamite. He told her to tell the pilot to stay airborne until the parachutes and money was ready in Seattle – she then hurried straight back to the cockpit to relay the latest message.

Captain Scott told the passengers (who were blissfully unaware of the situation) that there was a mechanical problem which would require him to circle over Seattle before landing; although apparently ignorant of the hijacking, it would not have come as much of a surprise, as two-thirds of the 500-plus hijackings that have occurred worldwide over the last seventy-five years happened between 1960 and 1973.

Meanwhile, on the ground, the *de facto* crisis team were doing everything they could to get things moving quickly. Seattle police, FBI agents, Northwest Orient employees and FAA (Federal Aviation Administration) officials had roughly thirty minutes to meet Cooper's demands. The FBI were racing to get the $200,000 cash while the Seattle police worked to obtain two sets of parachutes. It was with these that Cooper's attention to detail became apparent

– he had demanded two backpacks and two chestpacks, but when authorities at McChord Air Force Base agreed to provide military-issue chutes, he declined: they had automatic opening mechanisms. Cooper insisted on civilian chutes, with user-operated ripcords. After a series of hasty telephone calls, Seattle police made contact with the owner of a skydiving school, who was met by officers at the school (which was shut at the time). Soon, a police car with sirens wailing was screaming towards Sea-Tac with its precious cargo of four civvy parachutes.

The $200,000 was to be sourced at random without sequential serial numbers. The FBI agents who were satisfying the request complied, but made sure that each serial began with the letter L and was issued by the Federal Reserve Office in San Francisco, with nearly all the notes dated from 1969.

However, there was something else about the $200,000 which really did point to Cooper's meticulous planning – the fact that he had specifically asked for it in $20 bills. A higher value note would have been suspicious whilst lower ones would have weighed far more, possibly preventing his safe transit to earth (of course agents did not know this at the time, partly because of the request for multiple parachutes).

Waiting for the team to fulfil his demands, Cooper drank a bourbon and water on board the aircraft, even offering to pay flight attendant Mucklow for it. Whilst the FBI have portrayed Cooper as 'boozy' and even 'obscene', Mucklow (who spent the most time with him out of all the crew) described him as 'rather nice... never cruel or nasty... thoughtful and calm.' One example was Cooper's request that meals for the crew be brought on board when the aircraft was waiting on the ground in Seattle. This man was certainly proving hard to please!

With everything ready on the ground, the crisis team radioed Captain Scott at 5.24p.m. with the simple message that 'Everything is ready for your arrival'. The 727 landed uneventfully at 5.39p.m., just thirty minutes behind its scheduled arrival time. As soon as it was on the ground, Cooper ordered the captain to taxi to a remote stand with lights dimmed to avoid police marksmen. He also specified that no vehicle should approach the plane and that the person chosen to deliver the 'booty' should do so unaccompanied – this really did seem a well-planned operation.

The Northwest employee drove a car to a point near the plane. Cooper ordered Mucklow to lower the stairs at the back of the aircraft, and the employee carried two parachutes at a time to them, where he handed them over to Mucklow. He then delivered the cash in a large, canvas bank bag. All demands met, Cooper allowed his thirty-six fellow passengers and attendant Flo Schaffner to leave the aircraft. He did not release Tina Mucklow or the three men in the cockpit; Scott, Anderson or Rataczak.

At this point, an FAA employee requested to come aboard via Captain Scott, apparently wishing to warn Cooper of the dangers of air piracy and the potential death sentence which could follow it. He was told to stuff it.

Cooper then read the instruction card for the operation of the back stairs, which were lowered from the underside of the rear of the body of the aeroplane, by using a simple lever. Cooper questioned Mucklow regarding the stairs, and she said she did not believe they could be lowered during flight. Cooper told her flatly that she was wrong. Here, his apparent knowledge of aircraft and aerodynamics came into its own – he was indeed right and he knew it, as the aircraft could fly easily with a little fuel in the relatively dense air at 10,000ft at just 80 knots using 15 degrees of wing flap.

For this reason, that was exactly what he asked the pilot to do using the flight attendant's cabin phone. He told him not to exceed 150 knots and warned him that he was wearing a wrist altimeter so he could monitor their height. Cooper told the crew he wanted to go to Mexico City, but First Officer Rataczak said the jet would have a range of just 1,000 miles at the altitude and airspeed Cooper had specified, even if loaded to capacity with 52,000 gallons of jet fuel. Mexico City was 2,200 miles away so, after a brief conversation, they agreed to a brief refuelling stop in Reno, Nevada.

Cooper then ordered a full refuelling of the aircraft before take-off from Seattle, and this was slowed by a vapour lock. After fifteen minutes, by which time the aircraft should have been full, Cooper demanded a full explanation and made threats – the fuel crew hurried up when they realised they were easily within the reach of the explosion which would result from a large quantity of dynamite!

Meanwhile, the hijacker and cockpit crew negotiated the flight path. A route as the crow flies from Seattle to Reno was impossible at Cooper's requested altitude of 10,000ft. The aircraft would have to pass perilously close to several high mountain peaks, including Mount Rainier at 14,411ft, Mount St Helens at 9,667ft and Mount Adams at 12,276ft. Captain Scott and Cooper compromised on a standard low-altitude route, Vector 23 in the Jeppesen air navigational charts that passed safely west of the mountain range. This airway allows aircraft to maintain altitudes as low as 5,000ft without nearing elevated areas.

This settled, Cooper instructed the pilot that the cabin should not be pressurised – he knew that when he opened the door, if the cabin was pressurised then there would be a violent flow of air. A prompt departure took place at 7.46p.m., two hours and six minutes since the aircraft had arrived in Seattle. After take-off, Cooper ordered Mucklow into the cockpit with the rest of the crew – as there was no peephole they could only guess what he was doing.

At 8p.m., by which time the aircraft had reached its specified cruising altitude, a red warning light came on in the cockpit informing the pilot that the rear stairs had been lowered. Over the intercom, Scott asked 'Is there anything we can do for you?' The response was a brusque 'No!' – the last word ever heard by the crew from the so-called Dan Cooper.

At 8.24p.m., the captain noticed a small dip in the jet's altitude, followed by a correcting dip of its tail. He suspected the rear stairs had been lowered, causing the jet to change its altitude. Scott marked the spot, near the Lewis River, 25 miles north of Portland. The crew considered the possibility that Cooper had jumped, but they had no choice but to continue to Reno since there was no way to confirm the suspicion short of disobeying his order to stay in the cockpit – if he was still in the back then he could quite easily blow up the briefcase.

By 10.20, they had landed at Reno. Five tense minutes passed. Captain Scott spoke over the intercom. No response.

He cautiously opened the cockpit door. Cooper had vanished, along with his hat, briefcase, overcoat, booty and one set of parachutes.

This left them to deduce only one thing – that Cooper had left by the rear steps with both backpack and chestpack parachutes, as well as a sack of money tied to his body with nylon cords cut from spare chutes. He would have stood on that bottom step, in temperatures of -7° Celsius and high winds – the aircraft was travelling at 170 knots at the time. And then, he would have leapt into the darkness to be met only by mile-high mountains and the spiky tops of Douglas fir trees.

No one ever saw him again, and no one has yet been convicted, making this the only unsolved hijacking case in US history. The FBI has an ongoing file on the case, which now comprises over sixty volumes. A massive search operation was initiated the next day, Thanksgiving, but nothing was found: not even the bright yellow and red parachute that he jumped with.

One good thing did come of the hijacking, however. Some bright spark came up with the so-called Cooper vane (otherwise known as the Dan Cooper switch), which is a kind of aerodynamic wedge – it stops the rear door of 727 aircraft being opened in flight and has been compulsory on all such aircraft by FAA regulations since 1972.

If you do happen to come across Dan Cooper, take him along to the police station and claim your reward – the *Seattle Post-Intelligencer* offered $5,000 in 1973, whilst Northwest Orient offered a reward of 15 per cent of the recovered money, to a maximum of $25,000!

Concordski: why the Soviet Union's Concorde equivalent would never work

Undoubtedly, the most famous supersonic passenger aircraft is Concorde. It first flew in 1969 and has been grounded since 2003. However, it had a competitor. And, as with the American space programme, the competitor lay in the Soviet Union, which produced the Tupolev Tu-144.

At first, the 144 looked remarkable. It was the first supersonic passenger aircraft to fly, and could do so faster than Concorde, and being slightly larger meant that it could seat more passengers. However, where the 144 fell down was on its range: under 2,000 miles in supersonic flight – Concorde's was double that. In addition the Soviet aircraft could only carry 70,000kg fuel, whilst Concorde could take 95,000kg. Tupolev's design bureau was much further behind the Aerospatiale and British Aircraft Corporation engineers (who were designing Concorde) in many respects. The 144's engines were inferior, being less efficient and burning more fuel than the Rolls-Royce jets fitted to Concorde.

The 144 programme was also blighted by setbacks, even though the Soviet team made a number of attempts to obtain Concorde designs. In 1965, Sergei Pavlov (officially working as Aeroflot's representative in Paris) was arrested and found to have detailed plans of the landing gear, braking systems and airframe of Concorde. The Paris Air Show of 1973 was blighted by the crash of the second production aircraft, which killed six people in the air and eight on the ground. In 1977, Sergei Fabiew (another agent) was

The idiosyncratic cockpit might have given the aircraft interior a visual edge, but it failed to be an overall success. (Leonid V. Kruzhkov)

arrested and found to have the entire plan for the Concorde prototype in his possession. The plan was from the mid-1960s – an early development blueprint which would not have enabled engineers to come up with their own aircraft. However, it would have showed the Soviet engineers what the French and British were planning.

The Concorde team was by no means unaware of the foul play, and as such strategically deployed a set of fake plans with deliberate (fairly catastrophic) design flaws. Perhaps unsurprisingly, therefore, the design of the Tu-144 contained equally catastrophic flaws. These manifested themselves in distinctly inconvenient ways – for example, an ex-144 pilot called Aleksandr Larin recalled that on a passenger-carrying flight in January 1978, between twenty-two and twenty-four on-board systems failed. About eight of these were before take-off, but officials decided that the flight should go ahead due to the number of foreign nationals and journalists booked.

However, after take-off the failures continued at an almost exponential rate. Whilst en route (whilst the aircraft was flying supersonic), Tupolev's crisis centre predicted that front and left landing gear would not extend for landing and that the aircraft would have to be put down on the right set of wheels alone, whilst travelling at nearly 200mph. With the almost certain death for all on board, the political consequences would be tremendous. Whilst Soviet leader Leonid Brezhnev was being informed of the imminent disaster on the ground, the problems continued in the air. With the many failures which were taking place, a siren (with a strangely similar intensity and sound to a civil defence warning) sounded in the cabin after take-off which the crew could not work out how to turn off. Eventually, the captain ordered the navigator to commandeer a pillow from one of the passengers and stuff it inside the siren's horn. Whilst the noise was now suppressed, the source of the problem certainly was not.

Luckily, on approach the wheels did manage to extend and the aircraft landed as smoothly as was possibly for a Tu-144 (a video online shows how difficult even NASA's

The Tu-144's design team allegedly used stolen blueprints, which actually contained huge flaws and were circulated by the Aerospatiale/BAC design teams. Here, Tu-144 and Concorde are seen together at the Paris Air Show. Spot the difference? (James Gordon)

The Tu-144 has not flown since the late 1990s and can been seen at various museums. (Zimin Vasily)

best pilots found it to land the aircraft smoothly when the aircraft was given a brief new lease of life for tests in the 1990s).

The last passenger flights took place in the late 1970s, with the aircraft being pressed back into service during the 1980s for cargo flights and training for the Buran space programme.

Many of the aircraft have now been preserved in museums. Whilst most of the technical problems which faced the programme in the 1970s were solved during the following decade, financial and political problems in the Soviet Union prevented the 144 from ever achieving the success which it might otherwise have done: whilst there is talk of putting one aircraft back in the sky for special occasions, it would take a great deal of funding and commercial backing which in times of austerity seems somewhat unlikely.

Chairway to Heaven: 16,000ft on a lawn chair...

Very few people find fame at 16,000ft. Even fewer do so on a lawn chair. Larry Walters, a truck driver who felt that he lacked fulfilment, can lay claim to both.

Aged thirteen, Walters had had the idea to fly using weather balloons after seeing them up against the ceiling of an army surplus store. Twenty years later, having failed to become a United States Air Force pilot due to eyesight issues, the intention remained but the ambition was now stronger. The plan was to attach some helium-filled balloons to a lawn chair, cut the anchor, and then float above his backyard at a height of about 30ft for a short time.

As such, in mid-1982, using a forged order slip from his employer, Larry Walters and his girlfriend purchased forty-five weather balloons and eight helium tanks from a local balloon supplier on the pretext that the balloons were for a television advert. In the garden of his home in San Pedro, California, they were then attached to the chair and filled with helium. Walters donned a parachute and climbed aboard.

He took with him a pellet gun, some sandwiches, a camera and a chilled beer. When his friends, who were gathered for the launch, cut the cord, he ascended rather more rapidly than he had expected: soon, he was gazing down at the state from 15,000ft up. However, fearing that he might upset the balance of his contraption and fall out, he did not want to shoot any of the balloons.

The need to get rid of some balloons became ever more pressing as he drifted merrily into the approach corridor of Long Beach Airport. Walters was in contact with the

Today, others enjoy cluster ballooning in a slightly less make-and-make-do fashion. It can be undertaken perfectly safely with careful prior planning, but the author does not recommend it. (Chris Breeze)

CB radio service REACT (Radio Emergency Associated Communication) and asked them to get in touch with people on the ground. After forty-five minutes in the sky, he decided to shoot some of the balloons. Thankfully, he did this before dropping his pellet gun overboard – any delay and he would have met a rather earlier demise.

A slow descent followed, after which he got tangled in power lines and caused a blackout in part of Long Beach, California, for about half an hour. He landed approximately 10 miles from where he started, and was immediately arrested as soon as he freed himself from the cables and climbed down. The Federal Aviation Administration (FAA) were all over him for 'operating an aircraft within an airport traffic area without establishing and maintaining two-way communications with the control tower' and also 'operating a civil aircraft for which there is not currently in effect an airworthiness certificate'. The latter charge was dropped because the rule was not applicable to lawn chairs and the punishment for the former was reduced from a fine of $4,000 to one of $1,500 after appeal.

Asked by reporters why he had done it, Walters replied: 'A man can't just sit around.' Of course he was in fact doing just that: but sitting around in the Long Beach Airport approach corridor! He became something of a celebrity and was invited onto national television, including programmes such as *The Tonight Show* and *Late Night with David Letterman*. The lawn chair used was given to a young admirer named Jerry (it still sits in his garage to this day). Walters handed in his resignation as a truck driver to become a public speaker at events, however the fame didn't last and although he was involved in some watch advertising in the early 1990s, he still was not happy.

Walters was undoubtedly a somewhat troubled character and after giving up his job, he found solace in reading the Bible and hiking the San Gabriel Mountains. He also did some volunteer work for the United States Forest Service. The final straw for Walters came when he broke up with his girlfriend (a relationship which had lasted more than fifteen years) and was only finding occasional work as a security guard.

On 6 October 1993, he walked up to what he found to be the most beautiful part of the Angelas National Forest and shot himself. He was only forty-four years of age. No suicide notes were found, although he left a Bible with several passages marked at his mother's house, just before he committed suicide. Among them was John 16:32: 'Indeed the hour is coming... each to his own, and will leave me alone. And yet I am not alone because the Father is with me.' A sad end to an extraordinary life.

Going Through the Lights: the only way to fly a hedge to Kuwait (by accident)

As you will have inevitably seen from many of the other stories in this book, for all its glamour and adventure aviation is blighted with scoundrels and crooks – and with aeroplanes at their mercy, their escapades can become ever more elaborate. The aircraft reflect that as they change hands, generally to less and less prestigious owners.

One such Boeing 707 started life with Pan American in late 1963 as N723PA. Pan Am then sold the aircraft to Air Union AG of Switzerland in 1974, which in turn leased the aircraft to individual operators in Nicaragua and some other countries under the registration of N711UT (or with Swaziland or Yugoslav registrations as requested by individual lessees). When Richard Rashid Khan Sr leased the aircraft in mid-1979, he put it under the false Zaire (now the ever-beleaguered Democratic Republic of the Congo) registration of 9Q-CRY.

At his instruction, it was flown from Helsinki to Lasham in southern England for maintenance with Dan-Air. However, even after work was carried out on the aircraft it was still sixty-two defects short of what would be required to make it fit to fly – including problems with the main landing gear. After nearly a month at Lasham, Khan Sr was requested to move the aircraft and chose to do so to Bristol Airport at Lulsgate in Somerset. However, just before they were due to take off one of the generators failed – reportedly the compasses were also functioning poorly and neither HF radio worked.

After twenty days on the ground at Bristol, the time came once again to move on and on 7 October 1979 Khan's son Richard Rashid Khan Jr asked the flight engineer to travel to Lulsgate to help him fuel the aircraft. The engineer said this was unnecessary as it could be done on the day of departure – however, Khan Jr went ahead anyway and loaded 70,000lb of fuel, filling the centre tank entirely before putting the remainder in the main tanks – the wrong order for this operation. Whilst he had experience as an airline pilot, his American commercial pilot's license had been revoked sometime beforehand – given his slapdash manner, this is hardly surprising.

On the departure day, 11 October, a further 82,000lb fuel was loaded under the supervision of the flight engineer, and Khan Jr told him to do the take-off calculations. Sums from the Pan Am operations manual supplied with the aircraft showed that it would need about 2,300m to take off – even though Bristol's runway is only 2,000m long in total. However, Khan consoled him that the runway was nearer to 2,400m and this temporarily laid fears to rest.

They taxied out to the runway and read off all the checklists, but on repeated occasions the flight engineer received no replies to questions or requests, such as asking for a take-off briefing and later whether it would be a rolling takeoff or a spool-up of the engines against the brakes. In the case of the latter, Khan Jr replied by entering the runway and setting take-off power. That was when it all started to become rather interesting. As more and more of the runway disappeared behind the old 707, its speed was only increasing marginally. Khan Jr pulled the stick back only at the very end of the runway, and the old craft staggered into the sky.

However, seconds later a call came from Bristol air traffic control saying something along the lines of, 'Sir, do you know what you have done?' Khan Jr had no idea. The aircraft had lumbered out of Lulsgate and taken with it a section of hedge, half a tree and the majority of the runway lights. In return, it had left some of the honeycomb structures from its flaps behind. The ensuing flight to Kuwait was blighted by pressurisation problems as the leaky ship was letting air out. Meanwhile one of the transformer rectifier units (TRUs) failed, another malfunctioned and most of the engineer's instruments were, like the compasses, fully or partially unserviceable by the end of the flight.

On arrival at Kuwait, Khan Jr exited the aircraft fairly promptly, leaving the co-pilot and flight engineer to study the damage. Metal bars from the runway approach lights at Bristol were hanging out of the fuselage underside, which had much of the debris embedded in it. Another 3ft-long metal bar was protruding from a wing whilst both of the landing gear legs carried significant chunks of a tree, including branches and the top part of the trunk as well as a section of hedge. Further debris from the lights could be found in the air-conditioning bay, which was also badly damaged.

Before the onward flight to Bombay could take place (for that was the final destination), some serious maintenance had to be done; the flight engineer walked round to the Kuwait Airways hangars to try to get some help with temporary repairs. Holes were patched up and minor repairs were undertaken, whilst the engineer spent ten hours repairing the TRUs and working on the airframe itself.

It was nevertheless clear to the crew that the problems were not solvable through a patch job and would need

This aircraft had a somewhat dubious career in the hands of the Khan family. It is seen here at Lasham, shortly before departure to Bristol. (Michael Zoeller)

proper maintenance. And despite assurances by Khan Sr before departure from the UK that facilities for such work would be made available at Bombay, these were later denied and landing gear problems started to become acute – indeed, when the aircraft was based in Bombay several flights were made to the United Arab Emirates with the left set of wheels down simply because they would not retract. When questioned, Khan's replies were that the left wheels were fully and safely retracted, which startled air traffic controllers and made them wonder if they were hallucinating.

However, the general appearance of the aircraft together with the increasing frequency of the problems made UAE authorities become more interested in what Khan Sr was doing; he solved the problems with forged papers and licenses and with various bribes, some successful and some not. Soon another problem began to emerge for Khan Sr: a lack of air freight business around Bombay. Business and the associated money began to dry up. The flight engineer's salary became gradually less regular, and he became more desperate in his search for ways to return to the United Kingdom. Part of a strategy employed by Khan to make sure that the crew would not co-operate with interested third parties like the UAE authorities included saying that their salaries were always due tomorrow – and when he was able to, he would blame the engineer for technical problems, which of course meant the engineer would stay to get them fixed for the sake of his reputation.

Early one morning in early January 1980, the engineer was woken by a rushed and agitated Khan Sr, who told him to prepare the aircraft for departure to Sharjah. He arrived at the airport to find Khan surrounded by airport officials, but when he approached the group he was told to go away. Eventually, although somewhat hurriedly, the 707 departed captained by Khan Sr. It stayed in Sharjah until 25 January, whilst members of the crew had considerable arguments with the Khans about salaries and other problems.

On 23 January, the flight engineer had been told that departure was imminent and he should remain in his hotel. The destination was not specified – he was only told that it would be in Europe. The next day he was told to prepare the aircraft for the flight, and specifically ordered to check all filters as well as the oil quantity, and also to supervise refuelling. The take-off would be very early the next morning. At dawn the following day, everyone gathered in the hotel lobby: both Khans, their wives, a child, a hotel employee who wanted a lift to Europe and also the engineer. The destination was set as Luxembourg.

When they arrived at the aircraft, the flight engineer checked the landing gear and particularly the levelling cylinder on the left set of wheels as it was this that had been preventing retraction. After a bizarre and almost forced visit to the duty-free shop, the aircraft's engines were started with Khan Sr in the captain's seat. Warned that take-off must happen within fifteen minutes for the left gear to retract, a prompt taxi to the runway was followed by a swift rolling take-off.

About two and a half hours into the flight, the 707 was cruising at 33,000ft over Turkish mountains. However, the engineer noticed vibration and the illumination of the low oil light for engine number three. He pulled the throttle back but the vibration increased and the engine seized within a matter of seconds. The vibration reduced but did not stop after the third engine had shut down: the fourth engine was also shaking and it was losing oil fast. The crew shut it down before it had a chance to seize (as it inevitably would, losing oil at such a rate).

Meanwhile, the aircraft had been descending slowly due to the gradual loss of power and had reached 29,000ft by the time the fourth engine was shut down. Further descent could not be stopped and at 16,000ft, Ankara was chosen as the diversion airport – both Khans were looking distinctly pale by this time. Hypoxia and oxygen deprivation was becoming a problem amongst all the crew thanks to there being no oxygen on board: engines one and two could not keep the leaky aircraft pressurised and keep it flying simultaneously.

Engine two was also beginning to show signs of oil loss and vibration by this time, and there was panic on the flight deck after air traffic control went dead whilst giving a radar vector – it turned out that a ground failure had caused the outage but the crew suspected electrical problems on board. Five minutes later they were back and the approach was continued and the landing carried out with both remaining engines operating.

After landing, the flight engineer found number four's 35-litre oil tank almost empty. Engines two and four would turn by hand but with difficulty, engine three was properly seized and only engine one was in good condition. When he checked the oil filters, he found a lot more sand and metal pieces than should have got there 'by accident', and wondered what had gone on whilst he was forced to go and buy duty-frees...

The 707 remained at Ankara as a lot of people were owed a lot of money by the Khans, who managed to evade capture. However, in October 1981 a Lebanese Armenian named Sarkis Soghanalian was charged with fraud in connection with the aircraft, and did not contest an extradition warrant to the USA. He also faced a civil order for 'failing to deliver material under contract'. However, it later turned out that Soghanalian was reportedly the Cold War's largest arms merchant and the main supplier of weapons to Saddam Hussein's government in Iraq. Before his death in October 2011, he gained the name 'The Merchant of Death' –

probably fair given that he oversaw billions of dollars worth of arms deals to factions and states all over the world. In retrospect, it is therefore probable that the 707's main purpose was arms dealing in some capacity: either way, the 'Khans' got off relatively lightly.

Hyde Park Airport: the story which completely tricked the press

In the late 1960s, runway space at London airports was at a premium (as it still is). Heathrow was packed with British and international scheduled operators. Gatwick was full of charter airlines and some scheduled carriers. Southend was well used by aerial car ferries and shuttles over the Channel, whilst Luton was both small and inaccessible but was again a charter base. Stansted was an ex-RAF base which served as an alternative for carriers wishing to avoid the high costs of Gatwick and Heathrow.

In 1968 the Third London Airport Commission was set up, chaired by Eustace Roskill, a lawyer and vice-chairman of the Parole Board for England and Wales. The report which the commission compiled was based on a novel use of cost-benefit analysis. Whilst this new-fangled technique might have seemed modern and efficient at first, it soon turned up some problems. For example, a Norman church was famously valued at just £50,000: the cost of its fire insurance.

The greatest weight was given to the convenience of passengers, calculated by applying a per-minute value for any reduction in journey times to the combined number of minutes saved by the total number of passengers who might use the airport over a ten- or twenty-year period. The trouble with this was that saving just one second per passenger would add up over a decade or two – so easily accessible and geographically well-located sites were favoured even when they drastically increased noise and air pollution.

An anti-expansion campaigner named John Adams used the report's own logic to suggest a novel solution to the third airport problem: Hyde Park. Easily accessible from London and the City, it would be ideal according to the cost-benefit analysis which Roskill was employing. Adams' essay was picked up by the *Sunday Times* which ran an article on it – however, the tone used in the work was not

When the Manhattan Airport Foundation announced plans to build a new airport on Central Park, the *Huffington Post* fell prey and posted a story about the scheme on its front page. (Manhattan Airport Foundation)

picked up and the newspaper thought that Adams was being serious. Seeing all these calculations, they thought 'he must be right' and suggestions were taken at face value.

The approach path to Adams' proposed airport would run over Buckingham Palace and Westminster Abbey – as would the take-off line. Readers who are old enough to remember what jet aircraft sounded like in the 1960s will know that Buckingham Palace and Westminster Abbey would have been in for rather more than their fair share of broken windows. However, more surprisingly it wasn't just the *Sunday Times* which got tricked. The article prompted a letter from the late Air Vice-Marshal Don Bennett to the *Sunday Times* 'congratulating those who have had the courage to recommend an airport in Hyde Park' and informing readers that he had first suggested Hyde Park back in 1946.

London is not the only city to have had hoax suggestions for new locations for an airport. New York witnessed the surfacing of the Manhattan Airport Foundation in 2009. This venerable organisation stated its mission as: 'To provide New Yorkers with a viable and centrally-located international air transportation hub.' Which was a nice way of suggesting that Central Park should be concreted over and have a world-class airport built on top. It calls Central Park a 'blighted urban space' that needs to be 'reclaimed' and assures that Tavern on the Green will 'be given the option of applying for a franchisee lease in the concourse food court'. And once again, a media organisation got caught out. This time it was *The Huffington Post*, which even ran the story on its front page until it realised that the suggestions were in fact satirical.

It doesn't require a great amount of detective work to find out that the Manhattan Airport Foundation isn't quite what it says it is, as pointed out shrewdly by researchers at gawker.com. It has its office on the fifty-eighth floor of the Woolworth Building... which only has fifty-seven floors. Its website supposedly dates from 2006, but the domain was only registered in April 2009. Arianna Huffington, who reportedly personally managed the front page of *The Huffington Post*'s website, probably had a lot to answer for...

Drugs on the Runway: a novel (albeit unsuccessful) way to import cocaine

Lots of people have been very innovative in the ways in which they attempt to covertly smuggle drugs into countries. Christopher Barrett-Jolley's chosen method involved the graveyard of a parish church and Southend Airport. His attempt was described by many newspapers as 'astounding even by his standards'. The flamboyant businessman and pilot was known for his exploits in Sudan and Afghanistan, which generally involved breaching trade embargos and arms dealing for one side or another (or both).

He first earned notoriety through his live calf export business out of Coventry Airport in the mid-1990s. During one operation a Boeing 737 crashed (killing the five crew) and only narrowly missed a housing estate. On another occasion animal rights protester Jill Phipps was killed after being hit by a livestock lorry travelling to the airport.

Barrett-Jolley's home was besieged by protesters (or so he claimed) and he was arrested after being filmed firing an air rifle at them.

1996 saw a tour of Afghanistan in a rickety old BAC 1-11 jet which attracted front page media attention regarding the purpose of the expedition: arms running between Bulgaria and a warlord in the north of the country, apparently. In 1999, a Boeing 707 flying one of the dubious cargos crashed at Bratislava Airport in Slovakia – more allegations about arms dealing followed. Barrett-Jolley was later convicted of fraud after claiming that his Range Rover had been stolen – it had not; he was obviously somewhat hard up at the time. Aged fifty-five, Christopher Barrett-Jolley wasn't doing too badly.

However, in summer 2001 (by this time owing a lot of people a lot of money), he decided to go a step further. The plan was to fly a staggering £22 million-worth of cocaine into Southend Airport and then have a drug gang run out from the nearby graveyard and collect it from the runway. A Boeing 707 cargo jet was to be used for the job, owned by a Nigerian company called Koda Air (apparently in turn owned by a 'Nigerian prince', according to the *Daily Mail*) but managed by a Belgian management company called Red Rock Aviation. Initially, Barrett-Jolley and his brother-in-law Peter Carine flew the plane from Lagos to Belgrade on behalf of the company for repairs.

Once this was completed, they then chartered the aircraft themselves and over several months £55,000 was paid into Barrett-Jolley's bank account in Tiverton, Devon, from another bank in Manchester. When he told

This aircraft's bizarre exploits were over by the time it was photographed here, at London Southend Airport, in July 2002. (Mathias Henig)

Red Rock Aviation that he wanted to charter the 707, he explained: 'We are not permitted to disclose our clients' real names but for the purposes of this matter let's call them Air America.'

Red Rock was told that the destination had to remain secret and that even Barrett-Jolley would not know it until the last minute – the cargo was 'security documents'. Red Rock and Koda Air agreed to the charter on the condition that an employee of Koda, David Ogundipe, travelled on the flight. Because of the 9/11 atrocities, American airspace was closed to charter aircraft for quite some time. The 707 finally took off from Belgrade on the afternoon of

11 October 2001. After refuelling at Las Palmas in the Canary Islands, they flew on to Montego Bay (Jamaica) and landed there in the early hours.

Later the same day Customs and Excise in London received a phone call from a firm of solicitors in Birmingham acting on behalf of Balkans war veteran Nikolai Luzaic, who had been hired by Barrett-Jolley to oversee the security of the operation. He became an informer, and he called later from the Holiday Inn hotel in Montego Bay saying that an operation to smuggle 500kg of cocaine was under way.

Five days later, after refuelling and taking on cargo (five suitcases and a holdall containing a total of 271kg of cocaine were put in the forward hold), the 707 left Montego Bay at 3a.m. The value of such a hoard in Jamaica at the time would have been over £1 million. Meanwhile, Luzaic called Customs and Excise again whilst on board, saying that the plan was for a gang to run from the graveyard and collect the drugs off the runway. When the aircraft got to Southend, Customs were waiting. The group due to nab the drugs from the runway saw the activity and were apparently scared off. Barrett-Jolley and Carine were both sentenced to twenty years in prison.

However, Barrett-Jolley wasn't the last person to attempt to smuggle cocaine into the United Kingdom by air. In October 2011, a seventeen year old from London named Ayesha Olivia Niles was picked out by Customs officers at Miami Airport in Florida. She was found to have bags of cocaine stuffed into twenty-four boxes of cake mix. Whilst the amount was a slightly more modest 13.5kg, she still faces fifteen years in jail.

By the time Barrett-Jolley is released he will be seventy-five. Some people mellow with age... we'll just have to wait and see in his particular case!

Missing in Africa: the jet which could be almost anywhere on the African continent

In general, it is safe to say that many African airlines employ somewhat more elderly fleets than other international carriers.

N844AA – a Boeing 727 jet built in 1975 – was one example. Having been retired by American Airlines, it changed hands a number of times before being bought by the Miami-based Aerospace Sales & Leasing Co. In turn, this company had leased it to TAAG Angola Airlines. However, it had sat idle at Luanda Airport for more than fourteen months, accruing more than $4 million in unpaid airport fees. Subsequently, it was being converted and refitted for use by IRS Airlines... but before it could be used once more in airline service, something very odd happened.

On 25 May 2003, the aircraft was flown off from Luanda – apparently never to be seen again. This prompted a worldwide search by both the FBI and the CIA, and whilst nothing has yet been found, what they did manage to piece together was a story which even a gifted fiction writer would struggle to concoct. Ben Charles Padilla had arrived in Angola in March 2003, apparently to supervise work taking place on N844AA on behalf of the leasing company, which had the intention of repossessing the aircraft and then leasing it to IRS Airlines. As a qualified aircraft mechanic, flight engineer and light aircraft pilot, this made sense. But the mysterious happenings of 25 May certainly did not.

That morning, without any kind of permission or flight plan, N844AA's engines were started and it began to taxi towards the runway. When air traffic control tried to make contact, they could not as all radio equipment as well as the transponder was turned off. One report suggested that the aircraft had been making abrupt changes in direction during the taxi, and also when taking off – it speculated that this could have been due to some sort of struggle on board. Conflicting reports suggest that there was either one or more than one person aboard at the time.

Either way, Padilla has not been heard from since. His sister, Benita Padilla-Kirkland, told the *South Florida Sun-Sentinel* newspaper that her family suspects that he was flying the aircraft. They fear that he subsequently crashed somewhere on the African continent or is being held against his will. US spy satellites took photographs of remote airstrips all over Africa, but found nothing. A sighting at Conakry, Guinea, in July 2003 later turned out to be another ex-American Airlines 727, with registration number N862AA. It was re-registered in Guinea as 3X-GDM and based there until it was destroyed in the UTA flight 141 accident at Cadjehoun Airport in Cotonou, Benin.

And, as the BBC explained, 'African airports are littered with old planes that have proved too costly to maintain and keep in the air'... there are many Boeing 727s plying the air routes across the continent, so finding N844AA would

Lost: one ex-American Airlines Boeing 727, seen here before its disappearance. (Ryan Gaddis)

be no easy job – and, so far, not even a trace of the aircraft has been found. Perhaps it was used in the Zambian space programme (see page 40)?

Skydiving Smugglers: the airborne method of Latin American drug trafficking

Drug smugglers worldwide have historically done almost everything within their power to evade the authorities, from transforming camper vans into tanks to building their own submarines.

One method involves jumping from an aeroplane with the powdered cargo and depositing it on the ground – after which it is possible to walk away apparently innocent. However, as with so many schemes, it certainly isn't failsafe and many attempts don't go according to plan.

Andrew C. Thornton II was the head of a drug smuggling ring in Kentucky. Having had a privileged upbringing and a private school education, he signed up to the US Army and became a paratrooper. After retiring from this, he became a police officer in a narcotics taskforce – a job which would stand him in good stead for his future career path.

Having completed part of a law course at the University of Kentucky, Thornton began smuggling drugs – probably as a way to fund his studies. But bad turned to worse and he soon became embroiled in drug trafficking schemes, as well as gaining a conviction for possession of drugs. Soon, he was flying from Columbia doing drug deliveries. On 11 September 1985, he put the Cessna 404 he was flying on autopilot and jumped out of the aircraft with a parachute, night-vision goggles, Gucci loafers, $4,500 in cash and an army duffel bag containing 40 kilos of cocaine worth $15 million. He also had a knife and two pistols.

However, events didn't go to plan and he got caught in his parachute (which he opened too late) and plummeted down into a back yard in Knoxville, Tennessee – needless to say, he did not survive. The plane came down 60 miles away in Hayesville, North Carolina. Three months later, a black bear was found dead after it overdosed on the drugs which Thornton had dropped in forty plastic canisters. But he wasn't the only one to attempt the method.

In May 1986, Roger Nelson (owner of the skydiving school Skydive Sandwich) was charged with drug smuggling along with several others. On 4 March 1987 he pleaded guilty and attracted much criticism from the skydiving community because of the image which he inadvertently gave it, partly due to the high-profile nature of the trial in the press. However, it wasn't really greed which motivated Nelson in the smuggling. Proceeds from the operation were used to purchase better student equipment for the school and fund the hire of a C130 Hercules for the 1986 skydiving convention. But this wasn't cheap at $120,000 in ferry fees from South Africa, $3,000 per day (not including fuel) and a further $11,000 fee for the crew's accommodation. Many jumpers also supported Nelson: April 1987 saw *Skydiving News* magazine run an advertisement by his friends. It stated: 'Roger Nelson, we support you. We realise how much you have done for skydiving and now it's time to show our appreciation.' The advert then asked supporters and jumpers alike to write a character reference letter and send it to Nelson's attorney, Fred Morelli.

But even this didn't receive an entirely positive reception: a police officer wrote in and said, 'I've seen cocaine kill, partially because of smugglers like Mr Nelson. He gambled. He lost! Don't ask me for a cent.' Nelson was jailed for ten years for tax evasion, but served only five due to good behaviour. He was released in 1993 and went on to run Skydive Chicago until his death due to a canopy collision in 2003.

Sometimes, it is skydivers who are at the hands of the drug traffickers: in 1985, seventeen members of a parachutist club were killed when Colombian drug smugglers avenged the plane owner's failure to deliver a $592 million cocaine shipment. The single-engine Cessna 208 Caravan stalled on 29 September of that year, just three minutes after take-off from a private airfield at Jenkinsburg in Georgia, and nose-dived onto a rural road, killing sixteen skydivers and the plane's owner, David Williams.

Two weeks previously, Williams had parachuted on the same flight as a parachutist who fell to his death with 35kg of cocaine strapped to his back. According to a government drug agent: 'those Colombians were upset when they didn't get their shipment... they wanted Williams to pay for messing up.' He did so with his life, along with sixteen others. Drug dealing is a messy business, however you choose to do it. But jumping out of a light aeroplane and parachuting the forbidden fruit down to your buyer has to be one of the least efficient and most dangerous methods!

Sheffield, then Plymouth: how Britain throws away its airports

For any city an airport is a valuable economic asset. You would therefore be forgiven for wondering why two British cities have completely got rid of theirs, even within the last five years.

Before Sheffield City Airport opened, the city was argued to be the largest in Europe to lack an airport. A proposal for one was first put forward in 1968 – but there was a problem. Because Sheffield is built on fairly hilly terrain, there was not much space. This is not necessarily insurmountable: London City Airport (which opened in the mid-1980s) has a very short runway – just over 1,500m – but is a highly active gateway to Central London. So, in 1997, the airport opened. KLM (the Netherlands flag carrier) described its shuttle to Amsterdam as the most successful start-up route it had ever experienced.

Soon, flights were offered with a number of airlines to other parts of the UK (including London) and Europe. However, when 9/11 hit, apart from being a massive tragedy on a human scale, it was also a disaster for the aviation industry. Many airlines, especially small regional carriers which were especially hard hit, went bankrupt. By 2002, all the airlines which had served Sheffield (BA, KLM, Aer Arann, Sabena and Albion Air) had pulled out or gone bust; the situation was compounded by a lack of radar which reportedly caused many airlines to refuse to fly to the airport on safety grounds. By the time the last flight left, much of the terminal had been turned into offices.

Peel Group plans to expand the site into a business park, covering the runway and building over remaining green space. (Jason Nicholls)

This was not helped by the fact that the airport had been bought by Peel Airports, a subdivision of Peel Group, which also owned Doncaster Sheffield Airport (the former RAF base at Finningley) just up the road. So, whilst Sheffield now wasn't entirely without flights, they certainly weren't on its doorstep. Needless to say, without scheduled flights the airport became 'unviable', and was therefore shut at the end of April 2008. The opportunity of extending the runway and adding radar (which would have made the airport very attractive to prospective operators) was all but ignored and a major source of controversy was the opinion held by many that Peel Group did not market the airport effectively. The airport now thrives... as a business park. In fairness to Peel Group, Sheffield City was all but overshadowed by its much larger competitor, which has a runway long enough for the low-cost airlines to operate from and is not entirely out of reach from Sheffield; that said, the decision is less than convenient for the people of the city and remains controversial to this day.

However, Sheffield is not alone as a city which has discarded its airport. The other example is Plymouth, which lost its airport in 2011 despite an outcry from the public. Sutton Harbour Group, which took over operation of the airport in 2000, made much of securing the future of the airport. It demonstrated commitment when it set up Air Southwest in 2003 to replace British Airways' services, which ceased that year. Problems began to emerge in the late 2000s recession when Sutton Harbour's profitability was hit somewhat. In 2009, the shorter of the two runways was shut and the company invoked a clause in its lease which allowed the building of houses on the land. Reportedly, the sale of land raised £11.8 million, of which just £1 million was reinvested in the airport.

Soon afterwards, landing fees went up (they later became the second most expensive in the United Kingdom for general aviation aircraft in some categories). This would only encourage private pilots to fly to other airfields.

However, in May 2010, the sale of Air Southwest (the only airline to operate to Plymouth due to the short runway requirement) was announced. Eastern Airways took over ownership of the airline in September 2010; changes, not all for the better, then began at the airline. The Group Chief Executive of Sutton Harbour, Nigel Godefroy, who stepped down from his post in September 2011, said about the sale of the airline: 'We want to give it an opportunity to blossom in hopefully a safe pair of hands'... many would argue in retrospect that this was not to be the case. May 2010 also saw the closure of the London City route (which reportedly had very good passenger numbers). A steady decline was becoming clearer.

December of that year was another bad month: firstly, all five of Air Southwest's aircraft were sold at approximately £3 million each and then leased back – a standard trick in the aviation industry to solve any short-term 'cash flow problems'. Secondly, on 5 December (a time when lots of people are sorting out their Christmas travel plans), air fares were raised substantially... would this encourage people to use Air Southwest? Probably not, especially on the London Gatwick–Newquay route where Flybe was strong competition (with the added advantage of being a huge regional airline in comparison).

Perhaps unsurprisingly, therefore, the Newquay/Plymouth –Gatwick route was dropped in February 2011, which caused the number of passengers going through Plymouth to drop below 100 per day (according to Sutton Harbour; this number is disputed). On 22 January, three aircraft had been put up for sale by the leasing company outright – did they know something that others did not? May 2011 saw the first aircraft leave the fleet for Australia, and the second aircraft departed for storage in Canada in July.

Plymouth Airport was a thriving hub with flights to numerous destinations in the UK and Europe. Here, a hangar has been bulldozed to make way for a housing development. (Piran Smith)

Charter operations were always a money-spinner for Air Southwest. Many airlines would lease aircraft when their own were unavailable including Aurigny (the Channel Islands-based airline) and Aer Arann (the Irish regional airline) amongst others. The latter airline operated a series of trial charters using Air Southwest aircraft out of Plymouth in 2008 to the Irish destinations of Donegal, Kerry, Shannon and Cork. Needless to say, the services sold out and went off full to the brim.

In April, the operations department at Air Southwest was closed. The next and probably the largest blow came when Sutton Harbour announced at the end of April that the airport would be shut by December at the latest. And, just five days later, Professor Peter Gripaios, an economist at the University of Plymouth, was quoted in the press saying that the closure was long overdue and 'it is time to think about other uses. It would be a good idea to have an Ikea or John Lewis on the site'. Of course, he chose to ignore the economic catastrophe which was losing the city's airport. Air Southwest then announced that all flights would end by 30 September.

On 6 July, Air Southwest announced it would transfer all its Plymouth flights to Newquay between 29 July and 29 August, due to the Plymouth Military Radar Station at HMS Drake being 'unavailable' during that period. However, airport manager Terry Linge confirmed that the station 'operates mainly during office hours' and 'closes down during the summer for staff leave; this has been the case for very many years' – he also said that the airport had run for sixteen years without this radar service (it was within range of others) in August and could operate perfectly safely without it. In reaction, Plymouth's Professor Gripaios (who had previously said that the closure was long overdue) said that the closure would make it 'much harder to sell the city to potential investors and the tourists' – an obvious contradiction to his previous comments.

Despite backlash from the public and the Save Plymouth City Airport campaign to which over 1,000 signed up, Plymouth City Council was more than reluctant to intervene (partly due to its not wishing to upset Sutton Harbour, which is a large employer in Plymouth), whilst the *Plymouth Herald* website allegedly deleted comments which were in opposition of the closure – and, in turn, comments relating to the deletion of comments. The organiser of the campaign to save the airport was reprimanded and later banned from posting comments altogether.

After airline services had finished, a final fly-in was organised for the weekend of the first two days of October to celebrate the eightieth anniversary of the airport and to bemoan its closure. There would be no landing fees (but a small donation to charity), a burger van and a lot of private pilots and aircraft. However, when Sutton Harbour Group got to hear of this, they reportedly viewed it as some sort of protest. They attempted to ban it, making the airfield strictly PPR (prior permission required) with slot times and other restrictions. The fly-in went ahead regardless, and pilots paid the full landing fee – willing to put up a stand (for a protest it now most certainly was) against Sutton Harbour.

The closure of Sheffield's airport was a shame; the closure of Plymouth's was a greater one, given its success until vested interests became involved. The people of Plymouth are now faced with at least an hour and a half of driving to either Exeter or Newquay airports, which is a costly journey in terms of both time and money given ever-rising petrol prices. The economic damage which the closure poses is untold. Yet airports continue to shut; Sheffield and Plymouth are by no means alone.

Despite huge protest, Ipswich lost its airport in the late 1990s even though commercial services to Manchester and Amsterdam had proved very successful, and even after lobbying in the House of Commons and a large sit-in: all this because the council decided that the site would be better used for housing. As you have probably noticed, this is something of a recurring theme with airfields. Rochester Airport (in Kent) is under continuing threat from the same problem, whilst Elmsett and Clutton Hill airstrips were saved from closure after a campaign from vociferous but minority local opposition.

However, Hanley William Airfield in Worcestershire wasn't so lucky and operations all but ceased in 2000. Manchester Airports Group (which owns Manchester, East Midlands, Humberside and Bournemouth airports) announced in May 2011 that it was 'reviewing the airports' it currently owned, saying that it 'sees a future for smaller airports in the UK' – probably referring to Bournemouth and Humberside. People don't realise how much of an asset an airfield is... until they lose it.

Sozzled and Slumbering: a rather unusual sleep disorder

If you're ever caught in a situation where you are absolutely trashed and really shouldn't be, don't worry. There's a good excuse.

The excuse in question was employed by American Airlines pilot James Yates in 2007, having turned up for duty nearly six and a half times over the alcohol limit. He was due to co-pilot a Boeing 767 aircraft from Manchester to Chicago with 189 passengers on board, but appeared for work dishevelled, ruddy in the face and apparently drunk. He was arrested after a positive breathalyser test and was taken to a police station, where another test showed up 129 milligrams of alcohol in 100 millilitres of blood (the legal limit for flying an aircraft being 20 milligrams in this case).

Yates was not charged with attempting to fly an aircraft while over the limit as he did not gain access to the plane – he only turned up at the airport to inform the flight captain he would be unable to perform his duties. He denied a single charge of carrying out an activity ancillary to an aviation function (acting as first officer) while over the limit. He was cleared.

But how did he manage it? The jury heard that he had been on a six-hour drinking marathon the night before (more afternoon really; it started at 4.30p.m.), so that hardly put things in his favour. However, Yates (of Ohio) suggested in the case that he may have drunk a third of a bottle of whisky *in his sleep* – even after going to bed. Attempting to explain why the bottle (which he had bought the day before) was now only two-thirds full, he said the drink had

Very few people manage to drink in their sleep, but one pilot managed it somehow. (Dan4th)

disappeared overnight, adding that 'strange things' sometimes happened in his sleep. The next thing he remembered after the spree was the plane's captain, Harvey Bell, hammering on his door at 9a.m. – just one and a half hours before the aircraft was due to take off. He was temporarily relieved of his duties and the aircraft was delayed whilst it stopped at New York to pick up a replacement crew.

Yates wasn't the only crew member to turn up for work somewhat tipsy. In November 2010, George La Perle turned up for work so drunk that he didn't know where he was supposed to be co-piloting his Delta Boeing 767 and its 240 passengers to. He was stopped by security officers after they smelt alcohol. He said that he had just had a few beers and was flying to New York. His destination was actually Detroit. La Perle was found to have 89 milligrams of alcohol per 100 millilitres (four times over the limit), and pleaded guilty to performing an aviation function with excess alcohol. Judge Philip Matthews described the consequences as 'potentially catastrophic' and sentenced him to six months in prison.

December 2009 had seen a similar incident, in which Shuttle America (operating on behalf of United Express) pilot Aaron Cope (thirty-three) turned up to co-pilot an aircraft from Austin (Texas) to Denver (Colorado). This time, the flight went ahead as normal and the captain, Robert Obodzinski, detected nothing untoward except for an odd odour periodically throughout the flight. After they arrived at the gate at Denver, Obodzinski leaned over and 'took a big whiff' – and, as he so eloquently put it, 'the smell of an alcoholic beverage was emanating from Cope'. The captain testified that whilst his first officer was able to speak and think apparently clearly, Cope certainly smelled of alcohol.

Whilst the first officer was carrying out the post-flight inspection, Obodzinski phoned the chief pilot of the airline, his union representative, and a Human Resources Manager for Republic Airways, the parent company of Shuttle America. He was directed by his company to escort Cope to an alcohol testing facility in the terminal building. The breathalyser indicated that he was severely over the limit, and he was sentenced to six months in a federal prison, followed by six months of home detention, the first three of which would be spent under electronic monitoring. Cope was also sentenced to serve two years on supervised release. Perhaps a harsh sentence, but it certainly makes it very clear that drinking then flying is not a clever course of action – if you don't run the plane into the ground then you'll certainly run yourself into prison.

Some years ago, the author's family was on a flight back from France, and as is standard the pilot came onto the intercom to give details of flight time and weather en route. His words sounded distinctly slurred to my father so he (much to my embarrassment) called the stewardess forward and asked her if the pilot was drunk at all. She replied: 'Not that I'm aware of; I'll check.' She went off to investigate and came back with an answer. He wasn't drunk, he was Dutch...

An Irish Mishap: we have now arrived at the (wrong) destination

A Ryanair flight from Liverpool to Londonderry (Northern Ireland); perhaps a little functional, you might think, but cheap flights are cheap for a reason. That is what the thirty-nine passengers probably thought on 29 March 2006 as they embarked upon their flight (operated by Irish charter airline Eirjet due to a crew shortage at Ryanair). The flight was fairly uneventful, until after touchdown in Derry, when the pilot apologised and announced 'we may have arrived at the wrong airport'. Everyone had a good laugh and thought it was a joke – perhaps they supposed that he was making reference to Ryanair's habit of landing people at airports rather further from their destination city. It was only when they glanced out of their windows to see army officers taking pictures that they realised that he was not joking. Meanwhile, the conversation between the pilot and City of Derry Airport's air traffic control went something like this:

> **Derry ATC:** 'Confirm your DME [distance measuring equipment reading].'
> **Eirjet aircraft:** 'We're on the ground.'
> **Derry ATC:** 'You've landed at Ballykelly.'
> **Eirjet aircraft:** 'I know.'

Passengers had to sit in the aircraft and wait for twenty minutes as steps were transported from Derry's main airport. Soldiers then climbed aboard and everyone had a bit of a laugh... except the pilots. And for good reason: the Airbus A320 (a 180-seater jet) had just touched down on

When Ryanair chartered an Eirjet plane to fly passengers from Liverpool to Londonderry, things went very wrong and it landed at a military base. (Press Association)

a runway meant for Army Air Corps helicopters, which had not been used by any large aircraft since 1971. To the amateur it might have looked fairly similar – one long strip of tarmac – if it weren't for the railway line which runs across it! This fairly distinguishing feature was apparently missed by the pilots, who had landed at a strip which was 6 miles from Derry's airport. None of the runways at Ballykelly have clear markings, except for white crosses which denote unsuitability for aircraft operations (other than a short 600m strip in the middle – a distance normally far too small to safely land an A320 in).

All that, put together with a distance reading which was 6 miles greater than it should have been and also air charts warning of possible confusion, was not enough to stop the pilots from landing the aircraft. Ryanair said in a statement that: 'In over seven years of Ryanair flights into City of Derry Airport, and over twenty years of Ryanair-operated flights, such a mistake has never occurred before.'

Needless to say, the pilots were grounded and then grilled by the UK's Air Accident Investigation Branch. However, the Irish Aviation Authority appeared to take a slightly more relaxed approach, saying that the incident was 'just something that happens'. Eirjet ceased operations in October 2006 due to financial difficulties.

However, as with so many of the scandals in this book, the cases aren't always exceptions. There have been at least sixteen such incidents between 2000 and the time of writing. For example, in 2005 a Spanair (operated by Nordic Airways) to Santiago de Compostela (in north-west Spain) ended up landing hundreds of miles away... in Seville (southern Spain). In 2009, a Northwest Airlines aircraft with 144 passengers from San Diego to Minneapolis went past the intended airport and continued flying at cruising altitude for another 150 miles before the pilots realised that they had overrun their destination. It turned out that they had become distracted on their laptops, and had not spoken to air traffic control for over an hour; thankfully the FAA revoked their licences, so you won't have to worry about having them in the cockpit.

Pay or Stay: when the passengers paid the fuel bill

When Comtel Air filled a gap in the market for flights between Birmingham (UK) and Amritsar (India), the link proved very useful for British Indians wishing to visit relatives. Advance bookings were good and flights were going off nearly full in each direction. However, only a short time after the route started, trouble hit the airline – and the airline hit the passengers.

In November 2011, nearly 200 passengers were flying back from Amritsar on Comtel Air. As was customary, the aircraft landed at Vienna for a technical stop – however, when it was expected to take off again, it did not. The Austrian airline had 'run out of money' whilst they were flying the first leg of the trip. A six-hour stand-off with airline staff followed, because the airline could not afford to fly the next leg of the journey and staff were asking passengers to fork out nearly £20,000 collectively (which apparently equated to around £150 per passenger) to pay for fuel and landing fees. Understandably, having paid their full airline fare already (on average around £550 each), they weren't having any of it.

However, because Comtel was an Austrian-registered airline, the UK's Civil Aviation Authority had no jurisdiction over it. What made matters worse was that Comtel Air was primarily an executive travel operator (it owned a Daussault 2000 business jet), and it was only leasing the Boeing 757 for commercial operations between the United Kingdom and India. Police were called to the stand-off which became increasingly tense until eventually passengers were escorted off the aircraft to cash machines, where they were forced to take out the money, although they were even given receipts of their new payments.

Reportedly, Comtel Air managed to rack up fines of more than £20,000 for not paying landing fees and taxes, which sent it over the financial precipice.

Meanwhile, Gurhej Kaur, a blind eighty-year-old grandmother from Handsworth Wood, was left on the plane for fifteen hours with no access to her medication, which was stuck in the hold. Reportedly, the office number on the airline's website was declared as 'not listed' on a recorded message, and the director of the airline only answered one call on his mobile phone in which he claimed that he would answer questions later. He then failed to take any calls, and the only person at the airline who could be contacted (claiming to be called Raj) giggled like a small girl when asked the question: 'Why do you treat your passengers like cattle?' and apparently replied 'Because they are!' When asked about the whereabouts of the director, he claimed that there was no point in calling the latter because he was 'probably gambling in the casino'.

600 passengers were left stranded by the collapse, and the 180 who were stranded in Vienna got back more than a day late – so it's good to know this supposedly luxury travel operator had its priorities in order. As one commentator quipped: 'Passengers made to have a whip round for fuel? Has anyone told Michael O'Leary?'

Plane Hoax: the plans without backing that bemused and bewildered

Earlier in this book was a story about a remarkable man who flew no less than 1 million miles without tickets and owes much of his fame to Stephen Spielberg and the film *Catch Me if You Can*. The subject of this story was not quite so adventurous but the tale is certainly as bizarre.

In 2009, a Yorkshire teenager calling himself Adam Tait approached a number of airports and airlines regarding his 'venture' – an ambitious low-cost carrier which was to be based on the Channel Island of Jersey and which would fly to much of Europe. As well as having a one-and-a-half-hour face-to-face meeting with Jersey Airport's director Julian Green, Tait, who told company bosses that he was in his twenties, also spoke with airlines including the Guernsey-based Aurigny, the Irish regional Aer Arann and the British charter airline Titan Airways. Whilst you might think these long-established companies were being rather naïve, there was a lot of credibility: Tait had bought up websites in the name of American Global Group, Island Airways and Channel Connect Airways.

He claimed that the supposed American holding company had a readily available fleet of twelve aircraft, expanding as demand required. Virtual offices with real telephone receptionists and bogus names had been set up, and all emails were signed off with 'American Global Group, 35 Countries, 22 Languages, One Team'. It got to the point where he was being chauffeured to Southend Airport in Essex by an air charter company from whom he intend to lease a ninety-three-seater BAe 146-200 regional jet. His intention was to inspect the plane and apparently to start the engines.

But it wasn't MI5 who would eventually bring this scam down. Nor was it the police who investigated the scheme. No private detectives had anything to do with foiling it either. Instead, a rather less likely candidate managed to unravel the ruse – and this particular organisation is not shrouded in secrecy, nor does it have any powers to tap telephones or read emails. No, it was *Airliner World* which was to be Tait's downfall. As one of the industry's leading magazines (it is in fact a fine publication to which the author is subscribed), Richard Maslen (editor) had tasked a freelance journalist to investigate the company. An extraordinary result presented itself. Seventeen-year-old Tait had achieved a remarkable feat: conning some of the more respected players in the aviation industry into thinking that his story was real – no doubts.

Adam Tait (his real name has been withheld at the request of his father due to ongoing mental health issues) had, according to his father, previously come 'within two days of bringing the American cast of *High School Musical* to a 300-seat theatre in Shropshire' and had only been foiled when queries arose on booking the hotel.

So if you have any doubts about starting an airline (lots of genuine people don't get as far), just get Adam Tait onto the board and you'll go a million miles... hopefully with tickets!

Premier Customers: how BA rewards supporters of Heathrow's proposed third runway

A suited passenger looking very important turned up at a British Airways lounge in Heathrow Airport, armed with a black British Airways Premier Card. An argument ensued between him and the lady behind the desk. She insisted that she did not recognise the card, and therefore refused him access to the lounge. He maintained that this was a perfectly valid card, which was 'somewhat more serious than Gold', and that she should check with her manager. After a short telephone call, she placed down the receiver, looked rather nervous, and let him through with much apology.

This must be one of the only occasions where a passenger who accosted a member of airline ground staff was right and got his own way. However, there was a reason that the attendant did not recognise the card: whilst she was neither badly trained nor uncaring about her job, she just wasn't aware of this mysterious black card scheme.

No one can earn the right to join through frequent flying. Reportedly, the issue of each individual membership must be approved by the British Airways board. Benefits include getting a seat on a full flight (so a commoner like you or me gets chucked off), and having one's flight held if one is late. Cardholders (there are reportedly less than 1,500 of them) are met on landing to enable them to be whisked through immigration without half the hassle which again you or I are forced to endure. They are also given a phone number to ring for 'special services', which include the tracing and tracking of lost bags and the fulfilment of special requests.

You are probably still wondering how you can join. The best way is to be the head of a large multinational company which supported the third runway at Heathrow. Or perhaps an influential politician – or maybe a member of a royal family... and those are only the easier ways!

Premier members include Sir Martin Sorrell, chief executive of the huge advertising company WPP, as well as Paul Walsh (one of the longest-ever-serving CEOs on a FTSE 100 company), chief executive of the drinks company Diageo and also John Connolly, who is chief executive of Deloitte. All three companies signed the joint statement in September 2008 that was influential in convincing Gordon Brown's government that Heathrow needed the new runway for the sake of the British economy.

Sorrell said about his membership: 'They look after you very well. It's the nearest thing you can come to having your own plane. If they have capacity, they will upgrade you from business to first'. However, BA has a slightly odd public position on Premier in that it says that the 'Premier Card system has been in place for decades' and that having a higher level rewards system is 'standard commercial practice', yet it also maintains a great deal of secrecy around the card – to the extent that there is no official page about it on the airline's website and only incidental mentions regarding lounge access (the words Premier Card appear only seven times in immediate succession throughout the entire site).

Perhaps most amazingly, the 1,500 members manage to rack up in excess of £1 million expenditure with British Airways annually – and considering that the cards are given to people rather than the companies of which they are in charge, that equates to each of them spending around £5,000 per year on BA flights. Maybe it was worth giving them that Premier Card after all...

Terminal 5: why did it all go so horribly wrong?

Costing £4.3 billion and six years after building had begun, Heathrow's shiny new Terminal 5 opened on 27 March 2008. The 36,584 passengers who turned up on day one were promised a 'calmer, smoother, simpler airport experience'. Sadly, that just didn't happen. Five hundred flights were cancelled, British Airways misplaced more than 23,000 bags (and made losses of £16 million) and twenty-eight lifts were out of order (and had never been in order). MPs called it a 'national embarrassment', and the fiasco reinforced the view of the House of Commons Transport Committee that BAA's monopoly over British airports should be broken up.

But what caused the problems? A combination of unfortunate issues had linked up to cause the 'Heathrow hassle'. In fairness to BAA, numerous tests and trials had been conducted whereby no fewer than 15,000 volunteers had created 50,000 'passenger profiles', which in all probability should have replicated nearly every possible travel scenario. 400,000 bags of different sizes, weights and shapes were put through the baggage handling system. The tests revealed very few problems – but that didn't stop BAA forgetting that just because they weren't revealed, it doesn't mean they don't exist. The price for this complacency was paid on 27 March.

Another issue lay in staff training. British Airways staff were given three days of familiarisation training to cover an area 'as large as Hyde Park', according to a BA employee speaking to the Transport Committee which investigated the failings. 'Two days out of the three were devoted to putting [staff] into a coach to show them x, y and z, and where to enter and exit', he said. In other words, there was almost no hands-on training whatsoever. The baggage area (where the problems occurred at opening) was a 'building site' during staff training periods, and they were only given a chance to get to know it during the last few weeks.

300 anti-expansion protesters besieging the building made matters worse – however, this faded into insignificance when compared to the colossal IT issues which were experienced on day one.

According to *Computer Weekly*, staff could not sign on to the baggage-reconciliation system to begin with and bags had to be sorted manually, causing huge flight delays. Problems with the wireless network connections at some check-in desks meant that staff could not enter information on bags into the system using their handheld devices. However, the main problem took significantly more time to be discovered. During the testing of the system, which involved the passing through of 400,000 bags, technicians installed software filters which would stop messages generated by the baggage system being delivered to the real systems at other terminals at Heathrow which were handling genuine passengers. However, these filters were accidentally left installed and remained in place after the terminal opened.

As a result, the Terminal 5 system (which was well proved at airports including Amsterdam Schiphol) was unable to connect with other terminals' systems and did not receive information about bags transferring to British Airways (the sole operator at T5) from other airlines – so all passengers routing via London were delayed (whilst bags were manually sorted) or left without their bags. On 5 April – a week and a half after opening – the reconciliation system failed for the whole day. It told staff that bags had not been security screened so whilst they were manually checked, they missed their flights.

Meanwhile, the system did not recognise a proportion of the bags which were held within the T5 baggage system for manual sorting because of errors in the transmission of the airline's flight data between BAA and the IT contractor SITA. A lack of capacity on the terminal's servers exacerbated the problems.

It was now that a large vicious circle began to build. As the errors built up, more bags went unrecognised by the system. These then missed their flights and had to be re-booked onto new flights. The baggage handling system then froze after it was no longer able to manage the number of messages generated by re-booking flights. Staff were forced to switch off the automated re-booking system in its entirety, which in turn caused more delays from the manual processes which replaced the automated ones.

By 5p.m. on 27 March, British Airways was overwhelmed to the extent that it could no longer accept checked baggage. Passengers were told in the departure lounge that they would be leaving without it and anyone who had not yet checked in could choose between travelling without baggage or re-booking their flight entirely. Meanwhile, staff sorted bags manually – this arrangement happened every day until 31 March, during which time 23,205 bags had to be manually sorted. It was only on 31 March that BA's IT staff were able to track down the bug and get rid of it. After this, things started to get more slick and fast, as promised in the beginning.

Anyone who has been through Terminal 5 since then will know that BA now more than does justice to the flying experience. The author has used the terminal a number of times and has found the process to be a fast and easy one, generally not as stressful as going through several other London airports. So for all the fiasco, perhaps it was worth it in the end.

Lost without Trace? The passenger prop that 'disappeared'

Reports were sketchy – but that is generally the case with most reports from Puerto Rico. Nobody was quite certain as to what had actually gone missing. Some news agencies reported a twin-engined plane; others a three-engined one. Fox News decided to go halves and report a twin-engined Trislander – unfortunately in this case a compromise just wasn't going to work. That aside, the eventual story which filtered out was a mysterious one.

On 15 December 2008, a Britten-Norman Trislander (a seventeen-seater piston prop) had taken off from Santiago (Dominican Republic) and was reportedly heading for

Mayaguana in the Bahamas (conflicting reports claimed that it was due to then head to New York) with eleven passengers and one pilot (normal on this aircraft). As the crow flies, that is about 260 miles – the range of the Trislander is over three times that so this should not have been a problem. However, about thirty-five minutes later the aircraft disappeared from Caribbean radar screens. Some Dominican officials claim that the pilot issued a distress call, although this is disputed.

Travelling at about 150mph, the trip should have been completed within one and a half hours. However, the

It remains unclear whether or not this aircraft actually ditched into the sea. No wreckage was ever found. (Daniel Pimentel)

Trislander didn't turn up at its destination airport and authorities assumed it to have ditched into the sea.

As such, the US Coast Guard launched a massive search and rescue operation early the next day, after the news of the missing aircraft was confirmed. Two helicopters and seven ships with 100 rescuers participated in the operation, which was based on the island of Providenciales in the Turks and Caicos (a British overseas territory). The search was suspended late on 17 December due to very bad weather after not even a trace of the aircraft was found in the 5,300 square miles combed for wreckage.

Another source of confusion was who actually owned the aircraft. It was registered as belonging to Línea Aérea Puertorriqueña (more commonly known as LAP, a company which appears to have ceased trading in 2009). The US Coast Guard reported that the Trislander in fact belonged to a company called Atlantis Aviation. Other sources contained reference to Atlantic Airlines. However, the story got more confusing and indeed more sinister when it was revealed by a spokesman of the Asociación Nacional de Pilotos that the licence of the pilot had been suspended in October 2006 after he had been caught flying multi-engine fixed wing aircraft when his licence only allowed him to fly helicopters.

The owner of the airline, Luis Perez, later gave more details on what he thought had happened. The man who stole the plane was apparently an Adrian Jimenez, a forty-three-year-old former student of the Dominican Republic Armed Forces and also a former navy cadet. Luis A. Irizarry, the lawyer investigating the disappearance for Perez, said a legitimate pilot for the airline had flown the plane to the

AIRLINE SCAMS AND SCANDALS

Turks and Caicos island of Providenciales for a test-flight by a potential buyer. That potential buyer was supposedly Jimenez, who sure enough turned up – but had eleven other people with him.

This was where the story got really interesting. The pilot who had flown the aircraft to Providenciales was later suspended: it turned out that allegedly he had helped Jimenez load and balance the plane after the former told him that he had already bought the aircraft. The pilot then got suspicious about the eleven other people and refused to fly beside him on this 'test flight'. Perez's lawyer later told Fox News Channel: 'The information we have is that he was planning to take these people out and he charged $26,000 for each of them... I think they were illegals [sic] and they wanted to get into the US... Why didn't they take a commercial flight? Because they were trying to get in illegally.'

Relatives of those on board told the Coast Guard that the passengers' final destination was indeed New York. However, the FAA did not have records to that effect, which indicates that the flight was supposed to be 'under the radar'. Among those missing is a maid from the Dominican Republic named Rosa Tavarez, twenty-seven, authorities said. Acquaintance Maria Torres told reporters that Tavarez wanted to find a higher-paying job elsewhere.

As far as the author is aware, no wreckage has yet been found. The aircraft was flying in the Bermuda Triangle zone at the time, but for all we know it did indeed land somewhere in the United States and drop its human cargo. Jimenez would therefore be as wanted as he would be rich. A Britten-Norman Trislander (they're fairly distinctive-looking things) piloted by a very rich middle-aged man with a cargo of Caribbean workers isn't easily missed; you might even see it whilst scuba diving.

Old News: why United Airlines' value went down $1 billion in 20 minutes

All it took was an error at Google and an over-zealous employee of an investment advisory company for investors to wipe out $1 billion of United's holding company within just over a quarter of an hour.

On 8 September 2008, a reporter at Income Securities Advisors (a 'third-party content provider' to Bloomberg News) was scouring Google News for bankruptcies in 2008. Over the last few days, Google News' internet crawler (which scans around 500 news sites per minute) had been looking around the internet and indexing articles. As it was looking, it found one article from the *South Florida Sun-Sentinel* about the 2002 bankruptcy filing by United Airlines. This was undated, and as such it gave it the date of 6 September 2008. The employee found it and assumed it was a new article, and decided that Wall Street would want to know about a major airline declaring bankruptcy. So he posted it to the Bloomberg Professional service at 10.53a.m.

Panic ensued and six minutes later, Bloomberg posted a news article headlined: 'UAL Shares drop 33% at 10:58a.m.' However, they continued to fall – 15 million shares of United Airlines stock had been sold before trading on the stock was halted for an hour. Then, at 11.16a.m., Bloomberg posted a correction in several languages, highlighted in red on the company's monitors: 'UAL SAYS IT HASN'T FILED FOR CHAPTER 11'.

Meanwhile, phone calls had started to flood into the Florida investment firm which had posted the news in the first place. Once Richard Lehmann (head of the company) realised what had happened, he moved quickly – he called Bloomberg and had the antiquated story removed by 11.08a.m. About twenty minutes later, Nasdaq halted trading on the shares.

By the end of the day, trading had resumed on UAL shares and the price had bounced back up to more than $12 a share. But the chaos of 8 September had only confirmed how happy Wall Street was to dispose of millions of shares without any confirmation whatsoever, so even a rumour or a blog entry could influence traders. According to Google News, old articles do appear every so often – however, they rarely have such a profound effect as they did on that fateful Monday morning.

That said, United isn't the only airline which has seen massive fluctuations in its share price. On 3 October 2011, shares in American Airlines ended 33 per cent down on fears that the carrier might have to obtain bankruptcy protection. At one point, they were down 41 per cent; thankfully, this triggered an automatic halt in trading.

When Flybe floated shares in December 2010 (at a price of 295p per share), it had high hopes for raising capital to expand operations in Europe. However, less than a year later, share prices had fallen 80 per cent after two profit warnings and the introduction of a fuel surcharge. Luckily, at the time of writing, the outlook seems bright for Flybe and significant further falls are not anticipated.

What all this shows is that airline shares are highly volatile, and investors have the potential to make or break their portfolios with them. As such, at the slightest whiff of trouble the share prices collapse... which can become very unfortunate for the companies involved.

Fake Licences: when the people in the cockpit don't have a clue

Back in 1997, Thomas Salme was a slightly bored twenty-eight year old working as a maintenance engineer at SAS. However, he also had a pilot's licence – it was not one which permitted him to carry passengers for money, but working at an airline presented its temptations. When a friend offered to let him use the full-size flight simulator at night when the rest of the training centre was not in use, he couldn't resist.

Salme gladly took up the offer and used the simulator for two to three hours at a time about fifteen or twenty times over the space of a year and a half. One thing led to another and on a whim he applied to be a co-pilot at a real airline. Having seen what a basic pilot's licence looked like, he made himself a Swedish Air Transport Pilot's License (which allowed him to fly large passenger aircraft) out of white paper – even with a logo and all the trimmings. Whilst this wasn't even laminated and looked distinctly home-made, it passed as real because permits look different from country to country.

His application to Italian airline Air One was successful, and, along with experience with that airline together with other carriers in the United Kingdom and Belgium, Salme accrued more than 10,000 hours of flying experience before he was stopped in March 2010, just about to fly a Boeing 737 of Turkish airline Corendon from Amsterdam to Ankara. The airline had co-operated with police and even had a reserve pilot prepared to take over the flight. Officers, who were tipped off by Swedish authorities, entered the aircraft just before it was about to push-back from the gate and arrested Salme. He pulled off his stripes immediately and was soon on Sky News justifying his actions – he said that he never put any passengers at risk but was ashamed to have lied.

In fairness to him, what he says is true: he did not put lives at risk. He passed all his line training and recurrent simulator checks without a problem, and nobody at any of the airlines he worked for is known to have any doubts about him... although it is never a comforting thing to see your pilot being led off your plane by police officers.

However, Salme is certainly not the only one to have faked his licence. 2011 saw a massive scandal in India, primarily involving pilots at the nation's flag carrier Air India and also the low-cost airline Spicejet. By mid-April, five people within the airline had been apprehended (some of whom are believed to have been pilots), and fourteen licences had been revoked because of false paperwork. This time, however, corruption was to blame.

A senior official in the Directorate General of Civil Aviation (DGCA) had been issuing false licences for fees – this led to the paperwork of nearly 4,000 pilots being scrutinised by the DGCA. Meanwhile, the Minister for

Civil Aviation (Vayalar Ravi) ordered an audit of all the forty flying schools in the country, after hours which had not been flown were being attributed to mark sheets. The plot thickened in August 2011 when the director of air safety at the DGCA was 'relieved of his duties' – it turned out that his daughter had been a pilot at Spicejet until she was sacked for falsifying documents... and it hardly takes a genius to make the connection. It turned out that he had indeed helped his daughter to a pilot's licence using his post at the DGCA – thankfully, the audit and checks on pilot details seem to have improved standards somewhat... that said, if you are sitting in the airport lounge waiting for a flight, and you see someone in a pilot's uniform with a pad of A4 and some colouring pencils, you should probably take the safer route or finalise your will before you take-off.

Snakes on a Plane stories from the Mile High Club

Believe it or not, there are many people who would really like to join the Mile High Club. If you don't believe it, talk to Mile High Flights who until recently operated a Cessna Caravan from Gloucestershire Airport especially fitted out with a sumptuous mattress and plenty of pillows; flying at 5,280ft, there was massive demand – until the Civil Aviation Authority suspended the company's licence in January 2011 saying that what goes on behind the curtain could be 'too distracting' for pilots.

Commercial aviation simply doesn't allow the space, and aircraft lavatories are hardly the most romantic of places, so many amorous couples (and, believe it or not, even a threesome) would go to Mile High Flights to get the full experience.

Branson did the deed when he was nineteen; he 'got chatting' to an attractive lady on a Freddie Laker flight to Los Angeles and things went a bit further. However, even he encountered problems: for one thing the woman was meeting her husband at arrivals so he had to hang back

Britain's very own dedicated Mile High Club service was grounded by the Civil Aviation Authority in January 2011 over fears that activities in the back could distract pilots. (Mile High Flights)

some distance; and the toilet cubicle in which they carried out their 'acrobatics' (as he described it) was so small that he remembered four distinct handprints on the mirror. With people banging on the door and very limited space, even Branson didn't enjoy the experience to the full – it makes one wonder about the choice of name for his own airline!

The space problem in aircraft toilets is one reason that some couples choose to do the deed in their seats and not bother with the loo – however, if you're sitting next to the participants it can get rather uncomfortable, as passengers on a British Airways flight from Brazil to London found out in January 2008. Olga Bezmelnitsyna was seen by a number of her 350 fellow passengers performing a sex act on her work colleague Sergei Gorlov about four hours into the flight, after they got 'carried away'. They were fined £500 each for outraging public decency. And whilst it is generally rumoured that a cup of cocoa before bed increases the libido, in this case it seems that coffee was to blame: they both were working for a tea and coffee company based in St Petersburg and had been in São Paulo to sample several different varieties of coffee beans.

So if you are planning on joining the Mile High Club, make sure you aren't a celebrity sitting next to someone who works for a tabloid... and if you lock the door and stay in there too long expect to have the door bashed down. The film *Snakes on a Plane* provides a valuable lesson about copulation in aircraft toilets: the couple engaged in such activity are sure to be the first to be killed by any escaped venomous snakes.

Ranting: where to and where not to

In June 2011, the airwaves went blue after a Southwest Airlines pilot's microphone got stuck on and he launched into a four-minute obscenity-laced tirade without realising that most of Texas could hear what he was saying. Captain James Taylor of Argyle in Texas spent the time complaining about gays, grannies, overweight people and unattractive women. Air traffic controllers, meanwhile, were unable to communicate with other pilots while the pilot in question was blissfully unaware of the havoc he was causing.

Here's an extract from his fume... I'll leave you to guess what to replace the asterisks with:

> There's twelve flight attendants, individual, never the same flight attendant twice. Eleven ******* over the top *****, ******* homosexuals and a granny. Eleven. I mean, think of the odds of that. I thought I was in Chicago, which was party-land. I don't give a ****. I hate 100 percent of their ****. Now I'm back in Houston, which is easily one of the ugliest bases. I mean it's all these ******* old dudes and grannies and there's like maybe a handful of cute chicks.

A frosty reply came from the controller: 'OK, whoever is, uh, transmitting, better watch what you're saying.'

The FAA later tracked the recording to Southwest Airlines, which in turn traced the pilot – who had most certainly got out of the wrong side of bed. He was suspended without pay, and came back after a written apology to employees at the airline. However, Taylor isn't the only unfortunate pilot who has had his microphone on at the wrong time.

In another incident, a captain was addressing the passengers regarding weather en route and expected arrival time; however, in the middle of the sentence he broke off with 'Oh ****!!!' The passengers then sat nervously in their seats for the next five minutes, waiting for the inevitable oncoming collision or for the engines to explode. Then the captain came back onto the intercom and explained that the stewardess had just spilled a hot cup of coffee all over him... the underwear industry no doubt experienced a significant boost that day. But if you do wish to fill four minutes of your life with a homophobic, ageist and generally obscene rant, make sure you keep the microphone switched off or your audience may be rather larger than you thought.

However, radio isn't the only place where you can get caught out... thirteen Virgin Atlantic staff were relieved of their duties in November 2008 after they posted messages on Facebook describing passengers as chavs, saying that aircraft suffered from cockroach infestations and that engines were replaced four times annually. The airline said that it was impossible for staff to 'uphold high standards of customer service... if they hold these views'. In fairness to them, if engines were indeed replaced four times a year then that would be a fact and not an opinion... Virgin management couldn't quite get their heads round this.

In an unfortunate coincidence the same week, online rants appeared from British Airways' staff at London Gatwick about Heathrow's Terminal 5. The latter group was set up by 'London Gatwick Ground Staff' and described the British

Airways hub at Heathrow as 'shambolic' (admittedly they were correct on this one; see page 109), called passengers 'smelly and annoying', and slammed 'stupid American accents'. They complained that passengers often put their boarding passes in their mouths before handing them to ground staff, and also had a go at 'celebrity passengers' who required special treatment.

Predictably, every employer said much the same thing – that the behaviour was not representative of their very hard-working staff as a whole and that the individuals in question would either be given a good talking to, or the sack.

1 MILLION FREE SEATS: an offer which really is too good to be true

You might not believe it if you travelled on them recently, but some people love Ryanair – one of the only airlines to accept payment in mountain goats (very useful if you're flying to Greece, according to CEO Michael O'Leary). However, if you want to take something as heavy as a goat in hold baggage, it is likely that you'll be better off flying British Airways; probably first class. To its credit, Ryanair is a highly innovative airline. However, only the most astute travellers check the terms and conditions online before travelling, where many somewhat elusive charges can be found.

If you've checked in online but forgotten to print your boarding card, Ryanair can charge you 40 euros. This can also be applied if the printout is torn, of bad quality or part of it is missing (this includes any advertisements at the bottom) – all this is determined by airline staff. If you accidentally get the name wrong on the booking, that can cost another £160 if you pay at the airport or another £110 if you make the change at home.

If you're fed up of the free-for-all seating arrangements favoured by Ryanair, then on the face of it their Priority Boarding is excellent – just £5 (on selected routes, you can also pay £10 for a reserved seat). However, it turns out that even if you've paid, they don't always let you board first. This is the case at around twenty airports throughout Europe, where passengers go by bus to the aircraft. Whilst priority passengers are boarded onto the buses first, this produces no knock-on on the aircraft boarding process so you have effectively wasted £5. Ryanair's head of communications, Stephen McNamara, described the issue (which could be seen as a breach of contract) as 'a trivial, non-issue'. Good to know they care.

Then there's the £10 admin fee which is charged per person per one-way flight (so two people on a return would pay £40) and 'relates to the costs associated with Ryanair's booking system'. And if O'Leary gets his way (in true Ryanair style), you'll soon have to pay a pound to spend a penny. However, after all that there is certainly an argument that you get good value for money. In November 2011, it was announced that Ryanair was intending to show pornography videos on flights. Passengers would be able to use a Ryanair app using smartphones or iPads. The airline would then gain revenue through the passengers paying to gamble, play games, watch films, or even view hardcore sex scenes.

When questioned about the idea, Michael O'Leary said 'hotels around the world have it, so why wouldn't we?' – however, Bob Atkinson, of Travelsupermarket, disagreed. In a statement which spoke for itself, he said, 'There may be a market for porn in hotels, but that's in the privacy of a room... It's wrong.'

Hosanna in Excelsis: the regional airline which God cared about... apparently

When Durham Tees Valley Airport lost its link to London Heathrow with BMI in early 2009, there was an outcry from the business community who patronised the route: it wasn't through lack of passengers that the link got slashed – a pair of slots at the heavily congested London airport is worth millions of pounds, which can be therefore better spent on a more lucrative higher density, longer range route with more passengers.

Then there appeared Middlesbrough man Victor Bassey to save the day: his plan was to get Excelsis Airways (his start-up carrier) off the ground by restarting the flights to London using seventy-eight-seater Dash 8 Q400s. He claimed to have worked for British Airways, as well as helping to set up the US low-fare airline JetBlue Airways. It all seemed quite plausible... until holes started to appear in the plans.

At first, the aim was to fly thrice daily into Heathrow – which then changed to London City Airport due to a dearth of landing slots at the former airport. However, the latter had not heard anything from Excelsis even only months before it was planning to launch. The plan at first entailed using Boeing 737 jets, but this soon changed. Whilst very few noticed them, the cracks had already started to appear.

Top management was hired through airline recruitment agency Wynnwith Group: Andrew Bray (pilot and manager at several airlines), Andreas Blass (previously in charge of Binter Canarias), Keith Hampton (a top manager in several large British airlines) and Steve Tarbuck (an aviation consultant who had worked in various posts). The recruitment company is still owed £70,000 and the executives were not paid a single penny.

They grew suspicious after meetings were held in McDonald's and the multiple assurances of capital (including a credit note for access to $16 million at the Bank of America – which was fake). Before the first meeting in a smart hotel in Middlesbrough, Andrew Bray had to give his credit card details as an assurance – which left him with a bill to the hotel for more than £1,000.

However, when it turned out that sections of the airline's website (designed by E-Stands for £9,000, still owed) were copied almost directly from Canadian carrier Porter Airlines' website, Bassey pulled out yet another influential backer, who would 'prove doubters wrong'. This time, it was God. He said: 'When the time comes, everybody will see. I have a big backer in God.' Of course, that put investor and staff confidence up to an all-time high. That was in late August. And, whilst Taiwan was suffering from the worst flooding for half a century (which killed 500 and injured 1,000) and swine flu was busy infecting swathes of our earth, Victor Bassey honestly believed that flights between Durham Tees Valley and London City Airport were high on God's priority list!

In mid-October, the twelve staff resigned en masse, claiming that they had never been paid and could no longer see any hope that the airline would work out. The Civil Aviation Authority at no time received an application to operate. In mid-August, a press conference had been called in which one journalist asked whether the management was actually being paid – 'the disdain was palpable'. Andrew Bray (head of flight operations) said, 'We're not doing this for free'. Little did he know...

However, by no means was it Bassey's first foray into fraudulent activities. He was jailed at Newcastle Crown Court in 2005 for three offences of theft, using a false instrument and obtaining by deception. Other convictions dated back to 1989, which included theft and obtaining property by deception. Even his own wedding in the perhaps appropriately named Spennymoor involved unpaid bills.

Excelsis effectively collapsed on 6 October 2009 when Bassey left the office (a recently acquired replacement for the council house from which he used to work) on the pretext of needing to talk to a Swedish airline official. He, his laptop and his telephone were gone and his newly employed PA handed back the keys and called that job a day.

All in all, Bassey defrauded people and companies out of approximately £125,000. He originally denied all eleven charges against him, but at the last minute guilty pleas were entered for eight out of the eleven: three of fraudulent trading, four of obtaining services dishonestly and one of possessing an article for fraud. Bassey was sentenced to two years residence at Her Majesty's pleasure (for release no earlier than December 2012), and would not be allowed to be a company director for eight years after that. Durham remains without its flights to London, but perhaps that wasn't such a bad thing after all.

Ivory Tower: when Washington had a nap

On the night of 23 March 2011, two aircraft landed safely at Washington's Ronald Reagan National Airport. Nothing unusual, you might say, considering that this happens over one million times every year.

However, what made the event significant was that these aircraft landed without any assistance from air traffic control. Just after midnight, a Boeing 737 operated by American Airlines and an Airbus A320 of United Airlines landed safely at the effectively uncontrolled airport. The reason for a lack of control was not an experiment to examine pilots' effectiveness without help from the ground. Both aircraft had made contact with an approach air traffic control facility about 50 miles away in Warrenton, Virginia, which is usually responsible for guiding aircraft between airports. When a plane nears its destination, the facility hands responsibility for it to the destination airport's tower.

These Terminal Radar Approach Control facilities (known as Tracons) guide aeroplanes on their approach within 30 to 50 miles of the airports. They provide

Some air traffic control towers are left unoccupied at night. Washington National was not supposed to be, but it might as well have been. (John Murphy)

instructions for pilots to follow regarding altitude, direction and runway heading and make sure there is enough space between flights. Once an aeroplane is within 5 miles of the airport, and below 2,500ft, the pilots are handed over to traffic controllers in the airport tower who provide the final information on wind speed and the traffic ahead, as well as clearance to land.

Nobody knew, at first, why the tower had gone quiet. The controller (the only person on duty in the tower at this time of night) responded neither to radio calls from pilots nor to phone calls from controllers elsewhere nearby. Allegedly, the pilots also used a 'shout line', which pipes into a loudspeaker in the tower, to try and reach the controller. The reason for the lack of response was simple: the controller had dozed off. The planes that landed without tower help were two of the last three inbound commercial flights expected at the airport until 5a.m.

In itself, this is not abnormal. Billie Vincent, a former security director for the FAA, explained that many pilots have experienced landing at airports without a control tower. In fact, the vast majority of the USA's 19,000 airports do not have air traffic control facilities: they are often grass or dirt strips which simply don't need it. At these smaller airports, typically used for general aviation, pilots are responsible for logging into a specific frequency to broadcast their position and their intention to land.

But the controller (a comparative veteran in air traffic management having started out in 1990) wasn't just being lazy. It later turned out that he was on his fourth consecutive night shift – and that all the kerfuffle and controversy (generally involving whether or not he had been on drugs) which surrounded the story was completely unfounded. However, the fact that he was the only person in the tower at the time probably played a part.

Five years beforehand, Comair 191 turned onto the wrong runway at Lexington, Kentucky. The runway was too short, and the plane crashed on take-off, killing forty-seven passengers and two of the three crew members. There was only one air traffic controller – who had not had time to notice the aircraft's mistake until it was too late. The morning after the incident at Washington National, Transportation Secretary Ray LaHood announced that a second operator would henceforth be on duty for the night shift at the airport, and an investigation into the issue at other airports across the USA was proposed.

Perhaps it was the President of the National Air Traffic Controllers Association who summed it up most concisely: 'One-person shifts are unsafe. Period.' Needless to say, the controller was temporarily relieved of his duties whilst a thorough investigation took place. However, if you ever do find yourself circling to land over an apparently quiet airfield after a night-flight, you'll now know what the matter is.

Duty-Free the year-after-year prolific smugglers of the Orient

One airline in the Far East has managed to get quite a reputation – for smuggling. Everything from boxes of snakes to millions of dollars from drug profits (in Australia) has found its way around thanks to Vietnam Airlines' crew, even though the airline's policy is to sack anyone involved in such activities.

In March 2008, a fifty-eight-year-old pilot named Quoc Viet Lai faced no fewer than forty counts of money laundering after taking $3.7 million out of Australia between June 2005 and June 2006. But he was by no means the first – in 2007, another pilot had been arrested for trying to smuggle $300,000 into the country, and pilot Van Dang Tran was arrested in June 2006 when he tried to leave Sydney with lots of cash (reportedly $6.5 million) in his luggage. He was jailed for four and a half years.

On another occasion, Nguyen Duc Vu, a ground services officer working in Ho Chi Minh City's Tan Son Nhat Airport, was arrested in 2010 after it transpired that he had been paid $10,500 by two Vietnamese people in Australia to help them smuggle 'electronic goods' past Customs. In October of that year, Nguyen Quang Chinh, a maintenance worker at the Vietnam Airlines Engineering Company, was caught with some eighty new Canon digital cameras in a car at the same airport. The cameras (worth around $26,500) had just arrived from Tokyo's Narita Airport in Japan. In 2005, a multimillion dollar mobile phone smuggling scam was discovered.

However, within the airline the phenomenon has been going on for much longer. In May 2002, nine flight crew were suspended after items of jewellery and mobile phones were discovered on a flight from Dubai – Customs officers found them in plastic rubbish bags which were meant to be used for leftover food. The hoard included 7kg of gold rings and necklaces, along with some 400 mobile phones. In October 2006, another pilot (Pham Minh Tuan) was caught red-handed whilst attempting to smuggle 1.5kg of gold jewellery hidden in pilot's headphones to Russia.

Earlier that year, fifty-five packages (with a combined weight of 1,700kg) went unclaimed when they got to Russia after coming off a Vietnam Airlines flight. It turned out that staff had told airport workers to allow the bags on board (even though they were not checked by security and had an average weight of nearly 74kg each); whilst they were on the system as the bags of twenty-three passengers, the people who supposedly owned them were unable to answer questions about their contents. Forty-one of the packages contained labelled clothes and the rest had food in them, including dog meat (there is now a Facebook page against Vietnam Airlines crew smuggling dog meat overseas). It is thought some sort of arrangement had been made between the smugglers and the passengers, who agreed to carry the luggage as their own, and that the packages were supposed to be sold to Vietnamese workers in Russia. However, on arrival in that country, they went unclaimed and were returned to Vietnam.

In 2008, two flight attendants were suspended for illegally bringing $300,000 cash into South Korea. Nguyen Quy Hien and Nguyen Hoang Huong Xuan were caught carrying the money whilst going through Customs at Seoul's Incheon Airport after a flight from Hanoi. Later that year, another Vietnam Airlines pilot, Dang Xuan Hop, was arrested by Japanese police after landing at Narita Airport. He was accused of being part of a ring that smuggled goods stolen by a Vietnamese gang in Japan to customers in Vietnam. He denied knowing that the goods were stolen but admitted he received $100 for transporting the items each time – about twice a month for at least a year.

The airline has said that it is cracking down on smuggling by staff, and the campaign appears to have helped somewhat: at time of writing, no smuggling cases have been uncovered since June 2010, when a group of staff were removed from their posts after an incident involving the illegal movement of electrical items from Australia into Vietnam.

Too Saucy for Their Own Good: the sex scandal which ruined Cathay's marketing strategy

Sex scandals are quite strong stuff at the best of times... but when an airline is involved, the mixture is certainly a heady one. At the time of writing, the top suggestion on a popular search engine when typing in the words 'Cathay Pacific' is 'scandal'. Most unfortunate, considering that the airline is preparing to embark on a massive international marketing campaign.

The scandal in question is an unfortunate one: in early August 2011, photos surfaced online of a woman in a red outfit resembling Cathay's cabin crew uniform engaged in performing a sex act on a man (Chinese language newspapers reported that this was her boyfriend, a pilot for the airline) on board a plane. Whilst the likes of the BBC and the *Daily Telegraph* would not print the originals, the photos were blurry enough that there was no way to prove (or disprove) that they were taken whilst a flight was airborne. However, the photos made the scope for ridicule huge, one of the taglines being: 'Meet the team who go the extra mile to make you feel special.' The man would no doubt have been feeling 'special' enough, but the reputation of the airline has taken a veritable battering.

Chief executive John Slosar said that the two members of crew 'shown in compromising situations' in the photographs 'are no longer employees of the company'. The airline refused to say whether the incident took place in the cockpit, or whether the staff left their posts voluntarily. In retrospect, some would say that Cathay didn't handle the issue very well... however some airlines certainly know how to cash in on a sex scandal.

When US Rep. Anthony Weiner was embroiled in what has become known as Weinergate in June 2011 (in which he admitted to sending explicit photos of himself and carrying on inappropriate relationships online), Spirit Airlines managed to turn it into a commercial opportunity. As such the Big Weiner Sale was announced, featuring fares 'too HARD to resist', starting at the bargain price of just $9 each way. Maybe Cathay could have seen the funny side too. However, the airline hasn't exactly had an easy time in recent years – in 2008, the delivery flight of its first Boeing 777-300ER (worth somewhere around £100 million) was rather more spectacular than it was meant to be.

At 320mph, the jet flew just 28ft above the runway (at Boeing's factory near Seattle), with wheels up. It wasn't an emergency; just a stunt for senior executives on board (including British chairman Chris Pratt, CBE) performed by Captain Ian Wilkinson, who as chief pilot on the Cathay 777 fleet was described by the *Daily Mail* as 'one of Britain's most senior pilots'. Boeing employees and other spectators cheered as the aircraft turned a grey and dreary day into rather a thriller. Wilkinson was toasted with champagne on landing in Hong Kong, and his picture appeared in the airline newsletter raising a glass with the VIPs.

However, whilst the stunt had been approved by Seattle ATC, it had not been approved by the airline... which meant that when videos started appearing on the internet, they weren't best pleased. Captain Wilkinson was suspended, before a disciplinary hearing at which he was

Cathay Pacific has become bogged down in scandals over the last few years. (Miles-麥爾斯)

dismissed. Co-pilot Ray Middleton was taking orders from Wilkinson and was unaware that the fly-by had not been authorised; he was suspended from training duties for six months.

Muting on the Brown-ty: when a pregnant woman and a Red Cross doctor got downgraded for the ex-PM

Whilst it later turned out that somewhat sensationalist journalism was to blame more than anything else, the story which emerged in late March 2011 regarding Gordon Brown and his unfortunate upgrade on a British Airways flight from Oman caused quite a stir.

A pregnant woman, a Red Cross doctor and a number of other passengers were 'bumped' to less spacious seats and told this was due to overbooking, before Gordon Brown and his entourage boarded the aircraft at Abu Dhabi and sat in the better seats. This led the bumped passengers to believe that they were moved for the ex-PM and his aides... and when a tabloid newspaper got to hear of the story, all hell broke loose.

The pregnant woman got into a row with Brown's PA, Kirsty McNeill, after the former took a picture on her mobile phone of Brown asleep. When McNeill asked her why she was taking the photo, she replied that she was less interested in the ex-PM than why British Airways downgraded passengers because they were getting on the aircraft.

At this point, she was backed by the Red Cross doctor, who said that as someone who was 6ft 5in tall, he needed the extra legroom. He asked the PA when they had booked and if they really needed to fly in the higher class when he was downgraded to the more cramped seats, and if their tickets were funded by the taxpayer. After a good row, they all settled down and got some sleep.

Upgrades for the ex-PM and his entourage apparently separated a couple for ten hours, and caused a Red Cross doctor to be downgraded to economy class. (Scottish Labour)

The pregnant woman was separated from her husband for the ten-hour journey and it was for this that the airline refunded the couple £75 each, which they said was insufficient. After arrival in London, the *Daily Mail* was alerted to the story which was printed shortly afterwards and dubbed 'Mutiny on the Brown-ty'. The ex-PM's aide was described as aggressive and criticism was attracted from all sides. A British Airways spokesman said: 'It is very rare for a customer not to be able to travel in the cabin that they have booked... Gordon Brown and his party were booked in advance and were not involved in any way.'

The ex-PM's office reiterated this, saying that the arrangements were nothing to do with Mr Brown, who had booked his flight and seats well in advance and 'made no requests for – nor received – any special treatment'. The *Mail on Sunday* later printed an apology for the article, saying that 'neither Gordon Brown nor his staff received any special treatment from British Airways, nor behaved improperly in any way'. It apologised to Brown and his PA for the article and accompanying editorial, which had been somewhat uncomplimentary about his 'undistinguished time in office'.

However, whilst the apology was issued, no direct explanation was offered by British Airways or by Gordon Brown, which left readers wondering how the fandango had actually come about. Downgrading deserving people for an ex-Prime Minister and his aides has to be questioned in any circumstances... at least the *Mail* was satisfied that there was no wrongdoing in the end.

Je Veux Pisser: what Gérard Depardieu does when he just can't wait

You might recall that before take-off, aircraft lavatories are not generally available for use by passengers. In August 2011 Air France 5010 from Paris to Dublin was no exception, although the French actor Gérard Depardieu probably really wished it could have been. Whilst the aircraft was taxiing to the runway, he declared: 'Je veux pisser! Je veux pisser!' Whilst he was described by travelling companion Edouard Baer as 'stone-cold sober at the time', passengers' opinions on the problem couldn't have been further to the contrary. Nobody could have explained the problem better than the BBC, which said that 'Depardieu has a "oui" problem'.

Whilst he was desperate for a trip to the loo, it was locked as the Cityjet aircraft was just about to take-off. So as a last resort, Baer provided him with an empty Evian bottle into which he attempted to relieve himself as discreetly as is possible when one is urinating in a plastic container in public. Unfortunately, the bottle overflowed and its contents spilled onto the floor... a two-hour delay then ensued as flight attendants cleared up the mess, which Depardieu had offered to remove personally. However, he was thrown off the flight and told to re-book onto another one – not easy when you are due imminently on the set of *Asterix and Obelix: God Save Britannia*.

As he later explained in broken English to Anderson Cooper on CNN, 'It was so beautiful. I'm not a monster. I'm just a man who wants to pee.' The reason the bottle overflowed, he explained, was because 'I am an elephant... I have a lot of pee.' Whilst he made light of the issue, rather a different story emerged from Edouard Baer, who claimed that the actor suffered from prostate problems and that he was 'obliged to urinate'. He also denied that Depardieu had made any 'grand gestures' or shouted 'I'm going to piss'.

While Depardieu himself admitted earlier in 2011 that he could 'often behave like a complete a***hole' in public, the actor denied he was drunk – though he has also previously spoken of consuming five to six bottles of wine every day when stressed, or three to four when relaxed.

However, what was lost on swings to Cityjet was gained on roundabouts with Ryanair, which on its website offered fares of £9.99 (a price which really is too good to be true – see page 125) to passengers who were 'p***ed off with high fare airlines' – with two press cuttings explaining the Depardieu connection. However, the actor has certainly not been the only one made fun of by the Irish carrier, which at the height of the phone-hacking scandal promoted its sale fares for passengers 'hacked off' with high fares.

Depardieu had been expected in Ireland to join more than 300 cast and crew for work on the film (which had a budget of 50 million euros) at several locations including the Burren, County Clare, Listoke Gardens in County Louth and in Wicklow. Filming on part four of the Gaul's exploits began on the Tuesday following the incident and continued for four weeks – as far as is known, the return was thankfully somewhat less problematic.

Only a Practice attention, attention – the plane has not crashed!

'I can confirm that a 767 plane coming from London has had an accident at Harare airport... I am not at the site, but there are just injuries, no deaths. I cannot name the airline involved or say more at this particular time,' said David Chawota, chief executive of the Zimbabwe Civil Aviation Authority, late in the morning of 5 August 2010. It all matched up: Air Zimbabwe was the only airline operating from Harare to London and used Boeing 767s on the route. And knowing the flexibility of the airline's schedules, you can count on aircraft coming and going fairly randomly.

Major wire news agencies including Reuters and the Associated Press were quick to catch on and the news spread in minutes. Relatives of passengers in both London and Harare were worrying for their safety. A quick trip to the airport (if soldiers and armed police had not shut off approaches) would have revealed billowing smoke, police vehicles and ambulances galore.

But contrary to what the supposedly most responsible man in civil aviation in Zimbabwe had said, there was no accident. There were no casualties... it was all a drill. Even the head of Air Zimbabwe had been kept in the dark – to the extent that he told friends and relatives of passengers: 'We are trying to establish what has caused the accident. We have set up an emergency helpline desk to assist.'

The Foreign and Commonwealth Office was later able to confirm that the 'accident' was in fact a drill, and that the world's media had been tricked. The justification from

Chawota at the ZCAA was that 'Telling the media was part of the exercise. We wanted to see how the media would react' and that 'the drill was a success because all our systems worked perfectly. Police, security and hospital staff reacted swiftly.' Michael van Poppel who runs the Breaking News Organisation (another wire news agency which specialises in breaking news before other agencies even get to hear of it) said, 'he was lying to me when I spoke to him, but also to other reporters he spoke to... it was absolutely irresponsible of this CEO and I can't imagine what the families of passengers travelling to Harare around that time must have gone through when they heard news reports that there had been an "accident" at the airport.'

So if you do ever hear of an air accident in Zimbabwe, do check before believing what you're told – even the people in charge don't know.

Asleep in the Cockpit: how pilots who need more sleep get more sleep

As airlines push for greater efficiency and profits in a time of economic adversity, someone has to pay the price. At Ryanair, Michael O'Leary's view is that co-pilots would be better employed helping the cabin crew serve up tea and coffee when the aircraft isn't taking off or landing.

However, there is a more conventional solution which seriously impacts pilots, according to BALPA (the British Airline Pilots Association). BALPA commissioned a survey carried out by ComRes, a polling agency, with a 47 per cent response rate – 492 pilots – from one major airline. Of them, 45 per cent said that they suffered from 'significant fatigue', and one in five said that their ability to fly an aircraft was 'compromised' more than once a week. 43 per cent said that they had at some point fallen asleep in the cockpit unplanned, and 31 per cent of those said that when they had woken up, the other pilot was also asleep.

One pilot told the BBC that on one flight he fell asleep for ten minutes whilst his co-pilot was taking a scheduled break to have a power-nap. The plane could have been getting in the way of other aircraft en route to their destinations, the air traffic controllers could have been calling and not getting a response (this can indicate an incident like a hijacking) or the aircraft could have been going headlong into a mountain range. Thankfully, none of these things happened, but the probability increases substantially if there is no pilot at all.

In October 2011, a study amongst Swedish pilots showed that 70 per cent of them admitted to having made mistakes caused by tiredness, whilst 80 per cent reported that existing work hour rules 'constitute a threat to flight safety'. More than half admitted to falling asleep in the cockpit. One such incident took place in late 2010 on an SAS flight between the two Scandinavian capitals of Copenhagen and Stockholm. The captain recalled, 'I was extremely tired and had to fight to keep my eyes open' – however, he lost his battle after the co-pilot left the cockpit to go to the lavatory. When the latter attempted to return, he had to buzz at the door a number of times before the pilot woke up and let him in, and even after this, he was 'temporarily disorientated'. Whilst one's bed is a perfectly good place to come around after a nice snooze, the controls of a packed Boeing are hardly any good in this respect. No disciplinary action was taken, an acknowledgement by the airline that the pilot was not at fault.

In 2010, the final report regarding the crash of an Air India Express Boeing 737-800 (which killed 158 people) blamed a sleepy pilot's misjudgement. Having been asleep for nearly two hours, Captain Zlatko Glušica just wasn't thinking straight. Landing at Mangalore, the aircraft touched down 4,638ft along the 8,038ft runway – over halfway along. Regulations in India put the recommended touchdown point at 1,000ft or less.

However, if the pilots had applied full emergency breaking along with reverse thrust and the deployment of the wing spoilers, then 3,400ft would have been enough to stop the plane even with its high touchdown speed – and whilst a very expensive aircraft would have been wrecked, a disaster on a human scale would have been averted. Instead, they attempted to go around, applying full thrust with less than a kilometre to lift back off. The weather was fine and the wind was gentle but the fact that the pilot (and possibly the co-pilot) had been asleep was entirely to blame. Thankfully, the results are very rarely as catastrophic but the Air India Express incident shows what can happen.

The rules governing pilots' shifts are stricter in the United Kingdom than elsewhere in Europe, but these are under threat by the European Union's desire to standardise regulations across member states… which has led to pilots accusing the EU of giving in to airlines who want to cut costs. And if you think that it's just a trade union wanting easier jobs for its members, you'd struggle to find anyone who agrees with you at all – the European Aviation Safety Agency (the EU body in charge of aviation regulations within the community) found in a 2009 study that the current fourteen-hour shifts were excessive... yet it has so far failed to take any action on the matter.

So when you doze off on your long-haul flight, you can do so in the comfort that both your pilots might be doing just the same thing as well!

Epilogue

s you read this, my research on scams and scandals continues. In the (far) future there may be a second volume including stories of naughty goings-on during a manned mission to Mars, or perhaps of humanoid robots joining the Mile High Club when they should have been flying aeroplanes instead. However, it is probably more likely that I will have been incarcerated for supposed defamation and libel many years before any of that happens.

I hope that you have enjoyed reading this book: without using the old cliché of '...as much as I enjoyed writing it', it has certainly been interesting. Indeed, one particular Australasian bookseller believes that the product of my work is so racy that it requires a strict age range of 15+! Obviously, that's better than in some countries (which, to keep the reputations of their autocratic militaristic regimes completely spotless, will remain nameless) where being caught in possession of this book would earn you significant discredit with the ruling authorities and possibly even a public stoning.

My time leading up to publication of this book was in demand from many quarters; about one third of this book was written between the hours of ten at night and two in the morning! After that, the prose would become lumpy or I would slump down onto the keyboard and doze off; the word count of the morning after being deceptively gratifying, given that most of it had been written by my nose.

However, writing a book like this was also surprisingly difficult. From the start, it was not intended to be a heavy read and certainly not an air crash investigation book – most readers would agree that there is something distinctly unamusing about air crashes. And with the more juicy stories, I would have a responsibility to be slightly more discerning than many tabloid journalists on gauging what is tasteful and what is not. For that reason, several stories which were due for inclusion from the start were excluded after further investigation because they ceased to be even remotely comical thanks to their horrendous human consequences.

The airline industry is tremendously interesting but also amazingly prone to scams, scandals and scoundrels – fuelled by the glamour, the large sums of money involved and the inevitable thrill of flight itself, there are a considerable number of characters who serve as 'the enemies within' and a greater number who serve as the enemies without.

Happy flying!

Sources and Bibliography

'EasyJet's kosher flight meal – bacon', Robyn Rosen, *The Jewish Chronicle*, 17 February 2011, referring to Easyjet's Idea of Kosher: pork...

'EasyJet gives another non-kosher helping', *The Jewish Chronicle*, 24 February 2011, referring to Easyjet's Idea of Kosher: pork...

'Shock for BA cabin girls as sexy snaps posted on porn site', Brian Flynn, *The Sun*, 25 February 2010, referring to British Bareways.

'Montreal 'plane crash' a publicity stunt', Corinne Smith, CBC News, 26 March 2010, referring to Fake Crash.

'Fake 'Plane Crash' Staged For Publicity', Glenn Pew, AVweb, 26 March 2010, referring to Fake Crash.

'Flybe chief executive got £1m loan from main shareholder', *This is Cornwall*, 13 December 2010, referring to Loanshark.

'Flybe plays down £1m French loan', *The Scotsman*, 10 December 2010, referring to Loanshark.

'Unique flying school plan for Burn Airfield', *Selby Times*, 4 June 2008, referring to Waving Goodbye.

'WRAPS OFF SECRET AIR 'VISION' BID', *Selby Times*, 5 June 2008, referring to Waving Goodbye.

'World-class bid', *Selby Times*, 5 June 2008, referring to Waving Goodbye.

'Dead cow and a car engine amongst strangest items checked-in to fly', *Daily Telegraph*, 13 April 2010, referring to Cattle Class.

'Airline refuses to let weak-sighted passenger fly', *RT*, 23 February 2009, referring to Blind Ignorance.

'Airline rejects complaint from blind passenger', *RT*, 19 March 2009, referring to Blind Ignorance.

'Charleston Profile: Bona Fide★', Stephanie Hunt, *Charleston Magazine*, September 2010, referring to The Ultimate Skywayman.

'Zambia: Zambian astronauts train for Moon trip -- Interview with Space Academy Director', ITN Source, 14 November 1964, relating to The Zambian Space Programme.

'The Notorious Flight of Mathias Rust', Tom LeCompte, *Air & Space Magazine*, July 2005, referring to Cessna in Red Square.

'How did Concorde get its name?', *aerospaceweb.org*, referring to Concordeeeeeee.

D.B. Cooper: What Really Happened, Max Gunther, Contemporary Books (Chicago), 1985, referring to Great Plane Robbery.

D.B. Cooper: Dead or Alive, Richard Thomas Tosaw, Tosaw Publishing Co., Ceres (CA), 1984, referring to Great Plane Robbery.

'D.B. Cooper—Perfect Crime or Perfect Folly?', Richard Seven, *Seattle Times*, 17 November 1996, referring to Great Plane Robbery.

'D.B. Cooper, The Legendary Daredevil', David Krajicek, *TruTV*, 2008, referring to Great Plane Robbery.

'The Concordski project', Gerry Brooke, *Western Daily Press*, 2 March 2009, referring to Concordski.

'1993 At-Risk Survivor', Darwin Awards, November 1998, referring to Chairway to Heaven.

'Larry the Lawn Chair Pilot', Forensic Genealogy, 4 November 2007, referring to Chairway to Heaven.

'The Bristol Cowboy', David Learmount, *Flight International* archive, 27 December 1980, relating to Going Through the Lights.

'AIB reports on take-off by damaged 707', *Flight International*, 23 February 1980, referring to Going through the Lights.

'Who's behind the plan to pave Central Park and build an airport?', Leo Hickman, *The Guardian*, 24 July 2009, relating to Hyde Park Airport.

'Huffington Post Serves up Hoax on Front Page', Ryan Tate and John Cook, *gawker.com*, 21 July 2009, relating to Hyde Park Airport.

'Third London airport - in Hyde Park?', Richard (no other names given), Plane Stupid, 1 June 2008, relating to Hyde Park Airport.

The Manhattan Airport Foundation, referring to Hyde Park Airport.

'Final chapter in life and times of notorious pilot', John Revill, *Birmingham Post*, 6 December 2002, relating to Drugs on the Runway.

'Barret-Jolley – a life of crime', Jill Phipps Memorial, referring to Drugs on the Runway.

'African hunt for stolen Boeing', BBC News, 19 June 2003, referring to Missing in Africa.

'The 727 that Vanished', Tim Wright, *Air & Space Magazine*, September 2010, referring to Missing in Africa.

'Cocaine's skydiving smugglers', John S. Dermott, Martin Casey and Joseph J. Kane, *TIME magazine*, 21 October 1985, referring to Skydiving Smugglers

'SHG leader Nigel has decided to stand down', *Plymouth Herald*, 15 September 2011, referring to Sheffield, then Plymouth.

'Plymouth City Airport to close in December', BBC News, 28 April 2011, referring to Sheffield, then Plymouth.

'Plymouth City airport to close by year end', *The Guardian*, 28 April 2011, referring to Sheffield, then Plymouth.

'Drunk pilot George La Perle who didn't know where he was flying to jailed for 6 months', *Daily Mail*, 24 January 2011, relating to Sozzled and Slumbering.

'Pilot lands passenger jet at wrong airport', James Burleigh, *Daily Telegraph*, 30 March 2006, referring to An Irish Mishap.

'Plane lands at airbase by mistake', BBC News, 29 March 2006, referring to An Irish Mishap.

'Wrong airport landing explained', BBC News, 12 January 2007, referring to An Irish Mishap.

'Passengers had to pay £19k to fly home', *Express and Star*, 16 November 2011, referring to Pay or Stay.

'Comtel Plane Passengers Pony Up For Fuel As Airline Goes Broke', *Huffington Post*, 17 November 2011, referring to Pay or Stay.

'The airport hoax', James McLachlan, BBC Jersey, July 2009, relating to Plane Hoax.

'Teen duped airline bosses in real life 'Catch Me If You Can scam', Sarah Knapton, *Daily Telegraph*, 20 July 2009, relating to Plane Hoax.

'The airline concierge: smoothing out the seams for high fliers', Roger Collis, *The New York Times*, 31 January 2003, referring to Premier Customers.

'Premier Card', FlyerTalk, 3 August 2007, referring to Premier Customers.

'British Airways reveals what went wrong with Terminal 5', *Computing Weekly*, 14 May 2008, referring to Terminal 5.

'Owner – Missing Airplane Stolen by Fake Pilot, Illegal Immigrants', Rita Cant, *Fox News*, 19 December 2008, relating to Lost Without Trace?

'Mystery Deepens Surrounding Missing Plane Near Turks And Caicos', Aero News Network, 16 December 2008, referring to Lost without Trace?

'Mystery over lost Caribbean plane', BBC News, 17 December 2008, referring to Lost without Trace?

'Six-Year-Old News Story Causes United Airlines Stock to Plummet', Kim Zetter, *wired.com*, 8 September 2008, referring to Old News.

'A Mistaken News Report Hurts United', Micheline Maynard, *The New York Times*, 8 September 2008, referring to Old News.

'How a Series of Mistakes Hurt Shares of United', Miguel Helft, *The New York Times*, 14 September 2008, referring to Old News.

'2002's News, Yesterday's Sell-Off', Frank Ahrens, *Washington Post*, 9 September 2008, referring to Old News.

'Fake Swedish air pilot flies passenger jets for THIRTEEN YEARS without a licence... and is fined just £1,700', Mail Foreign Service, *Daily Mail*, 18 May 2010, relating to Fake Licences.

'Air India pilots bought licenses; 57 others showed up for work drunk', Rick Westhead, *The Star*, 23 March 2011, referring to Fake Licences.

'India's 'fake' pilots', Soutik Biswas, BBC News, 17 March 2011, referring to Fake Licences.

'CAA grounds UK's Mile High Club', Liz Moscrop, *lizmoscrop.com*, 2 January 2011, referring to Snakes on a Plane.

'Travellers get humped off flight', Thomas Whitaker, *The Sun*, 12 January 2008, referring to Snakes on a Plane.

'Flight of fancy', Tom Harvey, *The Sun*, 24 July 2007, referring to Snakes on a Plane.

'UK's only 'SleazyJet' service grounded', Aaron Sharp, *Click Liverpool*, 31 December 2010, referring to Snakes on a Plane.

'Southwest pilot apologizes for offensive rant against co-workers', *Overhead Bin (MSNBC)*, 29 June 2011, referring to Ranting.

'Virgin sacks cabin crew for insulting passengers on Facebook', *Daily Telegraph*, 31 October 2008, referring to Ranting.

'Virgin Atlantic staff fired over Facebook row', *The Argus*, 1 November 2008, referring to Ranting.

'Pilot suspended over "foul-mouthed rant"', BBC News, 25 June 2011, referring to Ranting.

'Southwest pilot rants and leaves his microphone on', JOE.ie, 26 June 2011, referring to Ranting.

'Ryanair's online check-in policy', *Daily Telegraph*, 11 March 2009, referring to 1 MILLION FREE SEATS.

'Victor Bassey – The truth behind the airline entrepreneur', Joe Willis, *The Northern Echo*, 17 October 2009, referring to Hosanna in Excelsis.

'Victor Bassey changed his plea to guilty', Joe Willis, *The Northern Echo*, 23 November 2010, referring to Hosanna in Excelsis.

'Air-link fraudster Victor Bassey faces prison', Gareth Lightfoot, *Evening Gazette*, 23 November 2010, referring to Hosanna in Excelsis.

'Middlesbrough airline fraudster's web of lies', Ian Reeve, BBC News, 20 December 2010, referring to Hosanna in Excelsis.

'Sleeping US air traffic controller suspended', BBC News, 25 March 2011, referring to Ivory Tower.

'Air traffic controller falls asleep, forcing planes to land unaided', Alex Spillius, *Daily Telegraph*, 24 March 2011, referring to Ivory Tower.

'Sleepy Air Traffic Controller: Was Shift Work to Blame?', Meredith Melnick, *TIME* magazine, 25 March 2011, referring to Ivory Tower.

'Vietnam pilot charged with smuggling drug cash from Australia', Associated Press, 31 March 2008, referring to Duty-Free.

'Vietnam Airlines staff arrested in smuggling probe', *Cargo Info Vietnam*, 24 June 2010, referring to Duty-Free.

'Vietnam Airlines official arrested for smuggling', Tuoi Tre, *Vietnews*, 16 June 2010, referring to Duty-Free.

'Sex scandal forces Cathay Pacific to review marketing strategy', *Daily Telegraph*, 15 August 2011, referring to Too Saucy for Their Own Good.

'Cathay Pacific scandal delays international ad campaign', BBC News, 16 August 2011, referring to Too Saucy for Their Own Good.

'Weiner scandal spurs Spirit Air's viral marketing campaign', Jessica Dickler, CNNMoney, 7 June 2010, referring to Too Saucy for Their Own Good.

'Pregnant woman is told to give up seat so Gordon Brown can fly in BA Club Class', *Daily Mail*, 25 March 2011, referring to Mutiny on the Brown-ty.

'How much are we still paying for Brown?', Fraser Nelson, *The Spectator*, 27 March 2011, referring to Mutiny on the Brown-ty.

'Gérard Depardieu's in-flight mishap', Marina Hyde, *The Guardian*, 18 August 2011, referring to Je Veux Pisser.

'Gerard Depardieu accused of urinating on floor of plane', Henry Samuel, *Daily Telegraph*, 17 August 2011, referring to Je Veux Pisser.

'Ryanair's latest controversial ad mocks Gérard Depardieu incident on Cityjet', *Terminal U*, 18 August 2011, referring to Je Veux Pisser.

'Zimbabwe Air Crash Drill: World Aviation Officials Did Not Know About 'Hoax' Accident', Alan McGuinness, Sky News, 6 August 2010, referring to Only a Practice.

'Zimbabwe safety drill sparks crash alert', Stuart Clarke, *Flight International*, 5 August 2010, referring to Only a Practice.

'Jetstar crews drunk with tiredness', Samantha Maiden, news.com.au, 12 June 2011, referring to Asleep in the Cockpit.

'Airline fires pilots asleep at the controls', Dan Glaister, *The Guardian*, 25 September 2008, referring to Asleep in the Cockpit.

'Northwest's Wayward Flight: Sleeping Pilots?', Randy James, *TIME* magazine, 23 October 2009, referring to Asleep in the Cockpit.

'This is your captain sleeping: How exhausted pilots snooze at the controls (and two of them even had a nap at the same time)', Ray Massey, *Daily Mail*, 7 April 2010, referring to Asleep in the Cockpit.

Index